ESSENTIAL MUSICIANSHIP

A COMPREHENSIVE CHORAL METHOD

VOICE · THEORY · SIGHT-READING · PERFORMANCE

BY

EMILY CROCKER

AND

JOHN LEAVITT

TEACHER LESSON PLANS BY
EMILY CROCKER, JANICE KILLIAN
AND
LINDA RANN

Essential Musicianship Consultants and Authors of *Essential Repertoire*
Glenda Casey
Bobbie Douglass
Jan Juneau
Janice Killian
Michael O'Hern
Linda Rann
Brad White

ISBN 978-0-7935-4332-8

HAL·LEONARD®
CORPORATION
7777 W. BLUEMOUND RD. P.O. BOX 13819 MILWAUKEE, WI 53213

AUTHORS

EMILY CROCKER
Vice President of Choral Publications
Hal Leonard Corporation, Milwaukee, Wisconsin

DR. JOHN LEAVITT, Composer and Conductor
Wichita, Kansas

DR. JANICE KILLIAN, Music Education
Texas Woman's University
Denton, Texas

LINDA RANN, Product Manager
Hal Leonard Corporation, Milwaukee, Wisconsin

CONSULTANTS

GLENDA CASEY, Choral Director
Berkner High School
Richardson Independent School District, Texas

BOBBIE DOUGLASS, Choral Director
L. D. Bell High School
Hurst-Euless-Bedford Independent School District, Texas

JAN JUNEAU, Choral Director
Klein High School
Klein Independent School District, Texas

MICHAEL O'HERN, Choral Director
Lake Highlands High School
Richardson Independent School District, Texas

BRAD WHITE, Choral Director
Birdville High School
Birdville Independent School District, Texas

PROJECT EDITOR
EMILY CROCKER
Director of Choral Publications
Hal Leonard Corporation, Milwaukee, Wisconsin

PRODUCTION EDITOR
RYAN FRENCH
Choral Editor
Hal Leonard Corporation, Milwaukee, Wisconsin

Send all inquiries to:
Hal Leonard Corporation
7777 W. Bluemound Rd., Box 13819
Milwaukee, WI 53213

CONTENTS

TABLE OF CONTENTS AND OVERVIEW OF THE PROGRAM

CONTENTS

CONTENTS

CONTENTS

INTRODUCTION

TO THE TEACHER

ESSENTIAL MUSICIANSHIP - BOOK 1 and the subsequent volumes 2 and 3 are designed to provide a basis for developing comprehensive musicianship within the choral rehearsal through a sequenced study of *voice, music theory* and the practical application of both in *music reading* skills.

For students to gain the most from this course of study, plan 10-15 minutes of daily study, including practice/review and introducing new material.

Features of the Program
- The sequence is pedagogically sound and practical. The necessary elements for good choral singing are systematically presented.

- The terminology is accurate and literal.

- Vocal pedagogy and music theory are presented in a format that is ideal for introducing important musical concepts within the choral rehearsal.

- The method is designed to help students become independent thinkers and to constantly apply their learning to an ever-widening set of musical experiences.

- It provides a ready-made resource of choral concepts and repertoire presented in a practical sequence that is ideal for both beginning and experienced teachers.

- It is designed to be successful within a variety of choral organizations: treble, tenor bass, mixed.

- The concepts presented are structured so as to allow students to discover their individual potential. The material is score-oriented, i.e., the students are led to discover the meaning of music both through experiencing it and interpreting it through the medium of the printed page. This process of converting "symbol to sound" and "sound to symbol" is at the heart of becoming a musically literate individual.

Combining ESSENTIAL MUSICIANSHIP with ESSENTIAL REPERTOIRE
This book should be presented in conjunction with any of the four levels of ESSENTIAL REPERTOIRE, twelve volumes of high quality, time-tested choral literature for mixed, treble and tenor bass choirs.

For each choral selection in *ESSENTIAL REPERTOIRE* there is a helpful student text page with background material, cultural context information, musical terminology, preparation exercises, and evaluation questions. In the Teacher Edition, the authors have provided complete lesson plans which include:
- Objectives
- Historical/stylistic guidelines and cultural context
- Choral techniques (warm-ups, exercises, drills)
- Rehearsal and performance tips
- Assessment techniques and enrichment ideas

Together with ESSENTIAL MUSICIANSHIP, these books provide a complete curriculum for the choral experience.

HOW TO USE THIS BOOK

ESSENTIAL MUSICIANSHIP - BOOK 1 is organized into twenty segments (chapters) each including material for developing skills in voice, theory, sight-reading, and performance.

The material in each segment has been systematically developed to integrate all the skills of a choral musician. How long to remain within a single segment will depend on a variety of circumstances, including the age and experience level of the students and how often the group meets.

Allow approximately 15 minutes of a 1-hour rehearsal to be devoted to the "voice/theory/sight-reading" portions of this material. This need not be approached as a block section of the rehearsal, but can be integrated throughout the lesson in shorter sessions to heighten the students' interest.

Each day's material should be balanced between review/practice and presenting new material. Before proceeding to the next chapter, evaluate the students' comprehension and mastery of the material.

Voice
Each segment provides material to help a young singer learn and apply the techniques of good singing, and particularly emphasizes the importance of:
• Good posture
• Expanded rib cage breathing, breath support, learning to sustain a phrase
• Tone production, choral blend, vertical vowel formation, diphthongs, word stress
• Diction, articulation of consonants

Theory
Each segment presents music theory concepts in a clear and concise manner. Appropriate drill is included and "check your knowledge" questions are presented in each chapter for a quick evaluation of knowledge-based material. Specific concepts are highlighted at the top of each page and in the table of contents/sequence overview on page iii.

Sight-Reading
The sight-reading drills and exercises are designed to allow the students to practice the concepts presented in the theory section of the chapter. Keep in mind that as the students practice particular drills they are internalizing that aural skill and synthesizing it with other musical concepts they have experienced.

The sight-reading drills include:
• Basic familiarity with musical terms and symbols
• Note identification
• Drills for echo-singing and group practice
• Combinable exercises that provide practice in unison sight-reading and part-singing

When working on the sight-reading material, always be musical when demonstrating and performing a particular phrase or pattern. Apply sight-reading skills in every area of music making.

HOW TO USE THIS BOOK
cont.

Methods of Sight-Reading

There are many good methods to use in developing sight-reading skills. For pitch reading, consider solfege (movable "do" and fixed "do") or numbers. For rhythm reading, consider Eastman, Traditional or Kodaly methods. They all have advantages and drawbacks. In selecting a method to follow, consider the following:

• Age and experience of the singers
• Methods used by other musical organizations in your school or district
• Methods familiar to your students
• Your own background and training

Remember, it is not *which* method you choose, but rather that it is employed consistently and daily. An overview of these common sight-reading methods for both pitch and rhythm are described in the appendix, beginning on page 186.

Performance

Each chapter includes repertoire that applies and reinforces the concepts presented in each chapter. These songs, written for treble, tenor bass, and mixed ensembles provide:

• Resources for developing reading skills, and the application of musical concepts
• Resources for developing musicianship and expressive singing
• Concert level repertoire that includes quality texts, a balance of styles, harmonic, melodic and rhythmic aspects of music-making (canons, counterpoint, expressive and satisfying melodies, speech choruses), and interesting musical forms
• A balance of repetition/patterning and experience with more challenging material

Music History

Throughout the text, short informational sections are included to help put the material presented into a historical context. This supplementary material helps students to see their own role as choral musicians now and as a part of a rich and rewarding tradition.

THE LESSON PLANS

Essential Elements

The Teacher's Edition of *ESSENTIAL MUSICIANSHIP - BOOK 1* includes objectives (Essential Elements) for the concepts presented in the book along with the corresponding National Standards for Arts Education.

Organization

Each chapter includes an extensive lesson plan which may be taught as suggested or modified as needed. Each teaching plan contains the following:

- A short chapter overview at the beginning of each of the twenty chapters, highlighting important new concepts to be presented and other helpful information.

- A reduced-size student page, with a suggested teaching plan in the margin.

- Essential Elements (objectives) correlated with the National Standards for Arts Education.

- Focus Statement — a concise, direct, statement presenting the most important expected learning. Many teachers will wish to write the focus statement on the board or overhead to direct the students' attention to the main outcome of the lesson.

- Teaching Tips — Suggestions for presenting the material in the student text, including sequencing information, suggestions for changing voices, and other special helps.

- Extensions — Where appropriate, the teaching plan includes ideas for extending the learning and other enrichment techniques.

- Higher Level Thinking — Choral music constantly requires students to apply higher level thinking skills. Suggestions are included for expanding students' understanding to new situations, especially in the areas of improvisation and composition.

- Special highlighted statements are included as appropriate. These are intended as friendly "teacher-to-teacher" tips and reminders, especially to help teachers of all levels of experience integrate the varied aspects of choral music within the daily rehearsal.

EFFECTIVE TEACHING CHECKLIST

Preparation
- Good planning leads to a successful rehearsal.
- Establish high expectations from the start – students want to succeed.
- Establish a routine and basic standards of behavior – and stick to it!
- Follow your planned routine every rehearsal (e.g. opening cue that rehearsal has begun, warm-up, sight-reading, repertoire, evaluation). Younger choirs in particular respond well to structure in a rehearsal.
- Plan, plan, plan.
- Develop long-range planning (the entire year's goals and activities, the semester, the month) and short-range planning (weekly plans and the daily lesson as they fit within the entire year's goals).
- Vary teaching strategies: modeling, peer coaching, large group, small group, cooperative learning, individual instruction, student conductors, independent practice.
- Study the score well. Anticipate problem areas.
- Be able to sing any one part while playing another.
- Know the vocal ranges of each member of the chorus.
- Select appropriate music to fit those vocal ranges.
- Remember: out-of-range results in out-of-tune singing.
- Select music of appropriate difficulty for the group.
- Plan evaluation techniques in advance.
- Have all necessary supplies and equipment ready (music in folders or ready to pass out, tapes cued, director's folder handy, recording equipment set, etc.) before the lesson begins.
- Plan to make beautiful music at least once during every rehearsal.

Presentation
- Begin each lesson with singing rather than talking.
- Make all parts of the lesson musical – including warm-ups and sight-reading.
- Rehearse a cappella. Use the piano as little as possible.
- Remember: Delivering information is not necessarily teaching.
- Display a positive attitude.
- Communicate effectively and concisely.
- Enthusiasm is essential.
- Make learning an enjoyable experience.
- Respect legitimate effort on the part of every student.
- Be the best musician you can be.
- Laugh often.

Pacing
- Be 30 seconds mentally ahead of the class at all times.
- Know where the lesson is going before it happens.
- Vary activities and standing/sitting positions.
- Plan a smooth transition from one activity to the next.
- Avoid "lag" time.
- If a "teachable" moment occurs, make the most of it.
- Avoid belaboring any one exercise, phrase, activity – come back to it at another time.
- Always give students a reason for repeating a section.
- Provide at least one successful musical experience in every rehearsal.

Evaluation
- Assess student learning in every lesson (formally or informally).
- Vary the assessment activities.
- Consider evaluating individual as well as group effort.
- Tape the rehearsals often (audio and/or video).
- Study the rehearsal tapes: 1) to discover where overlooked errors occur, 2) to assist in planning the next rehearsal, or 3) to share findings with the students.
- Provide students with opportunities to evaluate themselves.
- Teach critical listening to the students by asking specific students or a group of students to listen for a specific thing (balance of parts in the polyphonic section, a correct uniform vowel sound on a particular word or words, rise and fall of phrase, etc.).
- Constantly evaluate what's *really* happening. (We often hear what we *want* to hear!)
- Listen, listen, listen!

NATIONAL STANDARDS FOR ARTS EDUCATION
CHORAL PERFORMING GROUPS Grades 7-8
Essential Elements for Choir

The *National Standards for Arts Education* were developed by the Consortium of National Arts Education Associations under the guidance of the National Committee for Standards in the Arts. The Standards were prepared under a grant from the U. S. Department of Education, the National Endowment for the Arts, and the National Endowment for the Humanities.

Essential Musicianship, and the corresponding repertoire collections, *Essential Repertoire for the Young Choir (Mixed, Treble, Tenor Bass)*, are a part of the series *Essential Elements For Choir* and are based on these National Standards. In order to help teachers and students attain the National Standards, the authors of *Essential Elements For Choir* have developed related statements, more specific objectives, called *Essential Elements*.

By structuring this course of study around these Essential Elements and the corresponding National Standards, teachers and their students may begin to construct a vital relationship with the arts, and in so doing, as with any subject, approach this curriculum with discipline and study. The National Standards spell out what every young American should know about the arts, and the Essential Elements provide a framework for achieving these goals.

In the chart below, the National Standards (both *Content Standards* and *Achievement Standards*) are listed in **bold italic** typeface. The corresponding Essential Elements which are used in *Essential Musicianship* and *Essential Repertoire for the Young Choir* follow each National Standard in standard typeface. Throughout the text, each specific Essential Element is identified with the corresponding National Standard, i.e. *The student will sing with tall, uniform vowels (NS 1A).*

1. SINGING ALONE AND WITH OTHERS, A VARIED REPERTOIRE OF MUSIC
  A. Students sing accurately and with good breath control throughout their singing ranges, alone and in small and large ensembles.
  (1) Understand the vocal mechanism including parts and functions, and the changing voice
  - The student will describe and demonstrate the posture, breathing, vowel placement, and articulation necessary for good singing tone.
  - The student will develop an understanding of the vocal mechanism.
  - The student will develop an understanding of the breathing mechanism.
  - The student will build a repertoire of effective vocalises.

  (2) Develop and use correct singing posture
  - The student will describe and demonstrate good posture for singing.
  - The student will develop the posture and breath control needed to support choral tone through sustained phrases.

  (3) Develop and use correct breathing skills
  - The student will develop the diaphragmatic breathing needed to support choral tone.
  - The student will develop breathing techniques emphasizing the open throat.
  - The student will develop breath control adequate for performing melismas, crescendos, and supporting sustained phrases.

  (4) Develop good vocal tone, demonstrating proper breath support, vowel pronunciation, and placement/focus and head/chest voice
  - The student will discuss and demonstrate head and chest voice.
  - The student will discuss and demonstrate correct vowel pronunciation and tone placement.
  - The student will develop the posture and breath control adequate for performing melismas, crescendos, and supporting sustained phrases.

  (5) Develop proper diction through correct use of vowel shapes, syllabic stress, consonants, and diphthongs
  - The student will sing with tall uniform vowels.
  - The student will develop proper diction through the use of correct vowel shapes.
  - The student will discuss and demonstrate the neutral vowel (schwa).
  - The student will discuss and demonstrate the appropriate pronunciation of diphthongs.
  - The student will develop good diction through the precise articulation of consonants.
  - The student will articulate the "r" consonant correctly.
  - The student will develop clear diction to convey the meaning of the text.

(6) Develop intonation awareness
  - The student will aurally discriminate between in-tune and out-of-tune singing.
  - The student will practice good intonation.
  - The student will develop intonation awareness through the study of whole steps and half steps.
  - The student will develop intonation awareness through the study of the chromatic scale.

(7) Exercise responsible use and care of the voice
  - The student will develop technical singing skill focusing on the responsible use and care of the voice.
  - The student will develop an appreciation of the care needed for responsible use of the voice.

B. Students sing with expression and technical accuracy a repertoire of vocal literature with a level of difficulty of 2 on a scale of 1-6 including some songs performed from memory.
(National Standard 1B applies only to non-performing groups.)

C. Students sing music representing diverse genres and cultures with expression appropriate for the work being performed.
  - The student will develop proper Latin, French, German, Catalan, Hebrew, Italian, Spanish, and English diction through the correct use of vowel shapes and syllabic stress.
  - The student will sing choral literature from Africa, Italy, France, Germany, Spain, Mexico, Israel, England, Ireland, Russia, Scotland, and the United States.
  - The student will sing choral literature of various styles including spirituals, lullabies, folk songs from around the world, jazz, pop, and gospel, as well as traditional choral literature.
  - The student will sing choral literature from various time periods including Renaissance, Baroque, Classical, Romantic, and the Twentieth Century.

D. Students sing music written in two and three parts.
  - Students will sing choral literature written for unison, two-part, three-part, and four-part choruses.

E. Students sing with expression and technical accuracy a varied repertoire of vocal literature with a level of difficulty of 3, on a scale of 1-6, including some songs performed from memory.
(National Standard 1E applies to performing groups.)
Performance Activities
  (1) The student will perform individually, in small ensembles, and in large groups
  - The student will apply music reading skills to the performance of short accompanied or a cappella songs.
  - The student will perform in small ensembles for the choir, and where appropriate, for a wider audience.
  - The student will have the opportunity to perform solos, if desired.

(2) Articulating and practicing proper concert etiquette
  - The student will describe and demonstrate proper concert etiquette.

(3) Performance literature
  - The student will perform choral literature identified by such state and national organizations as the American Choral Directors Association, Music Educators National Conference, the Texas University Interscholastic League, the New York State School Music Association, the Wisconsin Music Educators Association, and others, as being of appropriate quality and difficulty for this age group.

Choral Ensemble Techniques
(4) Sing in tune through tone-vowel placement and careful listening
  - The student will increase his/her ability to sing in tune while singing harmony.
  - The student will improve intonation through the use of blended, supported vowels.
  - The student will listen carefully to rehearsal recordings, identifying areas of intonation weaknesses.

(5) Blend with other ensemble voices in areas of tone quality, diction, and intonation
- The student will demonstrate the ability to blend with other ensemble voices utilizing appropriate tone quality, diction, and intonation.
- The student will listen carefully to rehearsal recordings, identifying areas in which blend needs improvement.

(6) Respond to conducting
- The student will respond appropriately to conducting.
- The student will view rehearsal videotapes, noticing areas in which all ensemble members are not responding to conducting gestures.

(7) Pitch and rhythm accuracy
- The student will develop rhythmic accuracy by dividing the beat.
- The student will hold long notes for full value.
- The student will perform rhythms, syncopated rhythms, and changing meters with understanding and accuracy.
- The student will aurally identify areas in which pitch accuracy needs improvement and will attempt to repair those sections of music.
- The student will develop pitch accuracy over time through repeated practice.

(8) Demonstrate style characteristics (historical period, culture, dynamics, composer intent)
- The student will perform dynamic and tempo changes as indicated by the composer.
- The student will develop choral performance techniques of the Renaissance, Baroque, Classical, Romantic, and Twentieth Century eras.
- The student will become familiar with the musical terms which appear in each of the songs studied.

(9) Demonstrate phrasing (shape, movement)
- The student will aurally discriminate between musical and unmusical phrases.
- The student will develop the ability to musically shape a phrase.
- The student will demonstrate the ability to sing long sustained phrases while maintaining pitch accuracy.

(10) Demonstrate textual clarity (word accent, syllabic stress)
- The student will aurally discriminate between appropriate and inappropriate word stress.
- The student will demonstrate the ability to sing with appropriate syllabic stress.

(11) Demonstrate expression (sensitivity, mood, physical indication of feeling)
- The student will sing expressively as indicated by appropriate facial expression.
- The student will physically express sensitivity to the text.
- The student will verbalize the meaning of the text.

2. PERFORMING ON INSTRUMENTS, ALONE AND WITH OTHERS, A VARIED REPERTOIRE OF MUSIC
It is the purpose of this course in choral performance to emphasize the development of the voice and the choral art. Therefore, instrumental performance is beyond the scope of this text. It should be noted, however, that skill on a musical instrument, particularly a keyboard, is a definite asset for a singer/chorister and such skill should be encouraged at every opportunity. Choral directors should consider such choral and instrumental combinations as:
- Using student pianists as rehearsal and/or performance accompanists.
- Using instrumental accompaniments played by students.
- Highlighting instrumentalists from within the chorus on appropriate programs.
- Arranging joint band/orchestra/choir performances whenever possible.

3. IMPROVISING MELODIES, VARIATIONS, AND ACCOMPANIMENTS
A. Students improvise simple harmonic accompaniments.
(1) The student will improvise a harmonic accompaniment to the reading of a specified poem using an autoharp or other chordal instrument.
(2) The student will accompany an ensemble on guitar, autoharp or keyboard.

B. **Students improvise melodic embellishments and simple rhythmic and melodic variations on given pentatonic melodies and melodies in major keys.**
   (1) The student will improvise short melodies in C pentatonic on Orff instruments.
   (2) The student will improvise a pentatonic piece with contrasting sections.
   (3) The student will improvise pentatonic melodies using deliberate dynamic contrasts.

C. **Students improvise short melodies, unaccompanied, and over given rhythmic accompaniments, each in a consistent style, meter, and tonality.**
   (1) The student will improvise short melodies over rhythmic patterns played on classroom instruments.
   (2) The student will improvise on a given syncopated rhythmic pattern.

4. COMPOSING AND ARRANGING MUSIC WITHIN SPECIFIED GUIDELINES

A. **Students compose short pieces within specified guidelines, demonstrating how the elements of music are used to achieve unity and variety, tension and release, and balance.**
   (1) The student will compose rhythm exercises of quarter, half, and whole note patterns.
   (2) The student will compose a short composition in 2/4, 3/4, or 4/4 meter.
   (3) The student will create a musical composition using contrasting sections.
   (4) The student will compose and perform a rhythm piece.

B. **Students arrange simple pieces for voices or instruments other than those for which the pieces were written.**
   (1) The student will arrange a nursery rhyme or other familiar poem for speech chorus.
   (2) The student will compose a rhythmic setting for a tongue twister and arrange it for speech chorus and classroom instruments.
   (3) The student will arrange familiar folk or patriotic songs into a medley.
   (4) The student will arrange a familiar song in a contrasting style (e.g. from traditional to swing style).

C. **Students use a variety of traditional and nontraditional sound sources and electronic media when composing and arranging.**
   (1) The student will use music notation softward to notate a C major scale.
   (2) Students will create musical compositions on poetry by [Robert Lewis Stevenson] using computer generated sound or other musical sources.
   (3) Students will compose brief compositions using sounds available in the classroom.

5. READING AND NOTATING MUSIC

A. **Students will read whole, half, quarter, eighth, sixteenth, and dotted notes and rests in 2/4, 3/4, 4/4, 6/8, 3/8, and alle breve meter signatures.**
   (1) Read, write and perform rhythm patterns
   • The student will discriminate between beat and rhythm.
   • The student will echo-sing/chant/clap rhythmic patterns.
   • The student will read and perform quarter, half, whole, eighth note, and rest rhythms accurately.
   • The student will write quarter, half, whole, eighth note, and rest rhythms accurately.
   • The student will read and perform rhythm patterns in various meters.
   • The student will read and perform rhythms in changing meter.

B. **Students read at sight simple melodies in both the treble and bass clefs.**
   (1) Read and sing melodic patterns and harmonic structures in a variety of keys and tonalities, using specific methodology such as solfege or numbers
   • The student will read and sing rhythmic and melodic patterns in treble and bass clefs.
   • The student will read chord patterns in the keys of C, F, and G major in treble and bass clefs.
   • The student will read and sing melodic patterns using the tonic, dominant, and subdominant chords in treble and bass clefs.
   • The student will apply knowledge of whole and half steps.

C. Students identify and define standard notation symbols for pitch, rhythm, dynamics, tempo, articulation, and expression.

(1) Demonstrate knowledge of music theory including conventional and unconventional notation
  - The student will recognize and apply basic rhythmic notation (whole, half, quarter, eighth, and dotted notes and rests).
  - The student will recognize and apply knowledge of basic pitch notation (grand staff, pitch names, clefs, sharps, flats, and naturals).
  - The student will recognize and apply key signatures.

(2) Demonstrate knowledge of music theory by using music terminology
  - The student will become familiar with the musical terms found in specific songs included in the student texts.
  - The student will perform a piece of music utilizing the musical terminology indicated in the music to interpret the piece as suggested by the composer.

D. Students use standard notation to record their musical ideas and the musical ideas of others.

(1) Learn and use grandstaff, key and time signatures, pitch and rhythm notation
  - The student will describe and review elements of musical notation.
  - The student will recognize and apply basic rhythmic notation (whole, half, quarter, eighth, and dotted rhythms and rests).
  - The student will recognize and apply basic pitch notation (grand staff, pitch names, clefs, sharp, flat and natural).
  - The student will define pitch, scale, and key.
  - The student will recognize and apply key signatures.

(2) Learn and use scale systems, key relationships, and chord progressions
  - The student will describe the triad and the tonic chord.
  - The student will sing and recognize whole and half steps in major scales.
  - The student will describe and recognize intervals, chords, and triads.
  - The student will describe the concepts of measure, barline, and meter.

(3) Recognize musical forms
  - The singer will recognize and discuss musical forms, including: ABA, strophic, variation and coda.
  - The student will recognize and perform a musical example of canonic form.
  - The student will recognize form through repetition and contrast of musical material.

E. Students sight-read, accurately and expressively, music with a level of difficulty of 2 on a scale of 1-6.
(Applies to performing classes only)

(1) Sing and recognize intervals
  - The student will recognize and perform melodic and harmonic intervals.
  - The student will sight-read exercises which emphasize the tonic chord.
  - The student will recognize and perform harmonic intervals in an ensemble.
  - The student will practice singing melodic intervals in a short a cappella song.
  - The student will describe and recognize intervals, chords, and triads.

(2) Read and sing melodic patterns and harmonic structures in a variety of keys and tonalities, using specific methodology such as solfege or numbers
  - The student will sight-read short unison a cappella pieces.
  - The student will sight-read short accompanied unison pieces.
  - The student will sight-read short accompanied two-, three-, and four-part songs in the keys of C, F, and G major.
  - The student will sight-read short a cappella two-, three-, and four-part songs in the keys of C, F, and G major.

6. LISTENING TO, ANALYZING, AND DESCRIBING MUSIC

A. Students describe specific musical events in a given aural example, using appropriate terminology.

(1) The student will listen to a recording and describe the musical events in a specified choral work using the terminology with which he/she is presently working (e.g., describe the polyphonic entrances of soprano, alto, tenor and bass; aurally discriminate between examples of monophony, homophony and polyphony).

(2) The student will use appropriate terminology to describe recordings of his/her own performances.

B. Students analyze the uses of elements of music in aural examples representing diverse genres and cultures.

(1) The student will compare and contrast diverse types of choral music techniques (e.g. jazz tone quality vs. Renaissance tone quality, or dynamic contrasts in spirituals vs. that of the Baroque).

(2) The student will compare and contrast tone quality among diverse musical types such as traditional choral music, gospel music, country-western groups, ensemble music of China, and that of the Middle East.

(3) The student will discuss and analyze the musical characteristics of a madrigal, spiritual, or American folk song.

C. Students demonstrate knowledge of the basic principles of meter, rhythm, tonality, intervals, chords, and harmonic progressions in their analyses of music.

(1) The student will discuss musical elements, including meter and rhythm, present in a recording of choral music.

(2) The student will discuss musical elements, including tonality, melodic and harmonic intervals, and harmonic progressions of I, IV, and V.

7. EVALUATING MUSIC AND MUSIC PERFORMANCES

A. Students develop criteria for evaluating the quality and effectiveness of music performances and compositions and apply the criteria in their personal listening and performing.

(1) Critical Evaluation: Monitoring progress toward musical goals
- The student will monitor progress toward musical goals by noting development of his/her individual range.
- The student will monitor progress toward a musical goal by listening to early and more recent rehearsal recordings to note improvement in such choral techniques as intonation, vowel shapes, balance, and blend of the ensemble.

(2) Critical Evaluation: Evaluate self both as a solo and ensemble performer
- The student will listen critically to self and the chorus, concentrating on the balance and blend of the voice parts.

(3) Critical Evaluation: Evaluate self and others' solo and group rehearsals and/or performances
- The student will evaluate self as a solo performer by taping himself/herself singing at the end of the year as compared with the beginning of the year.
- The student will evaluate progress as an ensemble performer by listening critically to tapes, comparing polished performances with early rehearsals of a specific work.

(4) Citizenship Through Group Endeavor: Working effectively as a responsible team member
- The student will work effectively with others as a responsible team member by performing in small ensembles, creating original choreography in groups, and supporting efforts of the group through suggestions, encouragement, and enthusiasm.

(5) Citizenship Through Group Endeavor: Developing leadership abilities
- The student will develop leadership abilities by serving as student director, designing and teaching original choreography, leading a small ensemble, and acting as a section leader during rehearsal and/or sight-reading sessions.

B. *Students evaluate the quality and effectiveness of their own and others' performances, compositions, arrangements, and improvisations by applying specific criteria appropriate for the style of the music and offer constructive suggestions for improvement.*

    (1) Evaluate own and others' solo and group rehearsals and/or performances

- The student will evaluate his own and other's solo and group rehearsals and/or performances.
- The student will listen critically to self and the chorus, concentrating on the balance and blend of the voice parts.
- The student will listen critically to self and the chorus, concentrating on such choral techniques as intonation, diction, memorization, uniform vowels, and choral tone quality.
- The student will evaluate progress as an ensemble performer by listening critically to tapes comparing polished performances with early rehearsals of a specific work.

8. UNDERSTANDING RELATIONSHIPS BETWEEN MUSIC, THE OTHER ARTS, AND DISCIPLINES OUTSIDE THE ARTS

A. *Students compare, in two or more arts, how the characteristic materials of each art can be used to transform similar events, scenes, emotions, or ideas into works of art.*

    (1) The student will translate monophonic movement in music into monophonic movement in visual art or dance.

    (2) The student will combine history, drama, and music for an in-class presentation.

    (3) The student will combine the art forms of drama and music.

    (4) The student will combine drama, poetry, dance, and music to create a Shakespearean scene.

B. *Students describe ways in which the principles and subject matter of other disciplines taught in the school are interrelated with those of music.*

    (1) The student will relate a song based on the poetry of [Christina Rossetti] to language arts.

    (2) The student will apply language arts skills during music classes by listing different words which mean [pitch].

    (3) The student will apply information learned in music [anatomy of the breathing mechanism] to science classes.

    (4) The student will describe poetic imagery in a song.

    (5) The student will relate information about the ears, nose, and throat to issues of voice production and vocal health.

    (6) The student will relate music performed in class with events in American and world history.

9. UNDERSTANDING MUSIC IN RELATION TO HISTORY AND CULTURE

A. *Students describe distinguishing characteristics of representative music genres and styles from a variety of cultures.*

    (1) Hearing, identifying, describing, and performing music from a variety of musical styles, eras, and composers.

- The student will develop an understanding of the Western choral tradition, American spirituals, international folk songs, American jazz style, and the choral music of various countries through discussion, listening, and performance.
- The student will learn to sing in a variety of styles, (i.e. legato, jazz swing, Renaissance tone quality vs. Romantic tone quality, etc.).

    (2) Recognizing similarities and differences between choral styles of the major historical periods

- The student will recognize and describe similarities and differences among choral styles of the past and present.
- The student will perform literature and discuss characteristics of the Renaissance, Baroque, Classical, Romantic, and Twentieth Century eras.

B. Students classify by genre, style, historical period, composer, and title a varied body of exemplary musical works and explain the characteristics that cause each work to be considered exemplary.

(1) Recognizing similarities and differences between choral styles of the major historical periods

- The student will recognize and describe similarities and differences among choral styles of the past and present.
- The student will perform literature and discuss characteristics of the Renaissance, Baroque, Classical, Romantic, and Twentieth Century eras.
- The student will perform dynamic and tempo changes as indicated by the composer.
- The student will identify geographic regions and discuss the music from those regions.
- The student will compare and contrast music today with music of 400 years ago.
- The student will research music sung by persons of his/her grandparents' generation.
- The student will write an essay comparing popular songs of today with those of the Renaissance.

C. Students compare, in several cultures of the world, functions music serves, roles of musicians, and conditions under which music is typically performed.

(1) The student will explore careers in the field of music.

(2) The student will research (through books, video, and other media) the role of musicians around the world.

(3) The student will study how music is used in various cultures by researching, discussing, and, where appropriate, demonstrating a specified time or place (colonial America, African folk song, etc.).

EE1: GOALS AND OVERVIEW

EE1 includes the basics for beginning the course of study. While it starts at "square one", you may want to use it as a review chapter for choirs with more experience.

SPECIAL NOTE: *Essential Musicianship - Book 2* includes the same beginning material as *Essential Musicianship - Book 1*, but moves at a faster pace. Consider using Book 2 if your choir is older, more experienced or needs to move ahead more quickly.

The authors believe in the importance of using correct terminology, even with beginning ensembles. Present the concepts to your class using a variety of methods: the text, teacher presentation, teacher or student modeling, discussion, chalkboard, overhead projector, the keyboard.

Vary your methods of presenting the material. Make a daily, weekly, semester or yearly compilation of the musical terms and symbols which you regularly use in rehearsal.

ESSENTIAL ELEMENTS AND NEW CONCEPTS

Voice:
The student will develop the posture and breath control needed to support choral tone. (NS 1A)

- Posture
- Expanded rib cage breathing
- Producing a tone

Theory:
The student will understand beat and rhythm and be able to read and perform quarter, half and whole notes accurately (NS 5A, 5C, 5D)

- Steady beat
- Read and perform quarter, half, whole notes

Sight-Reading:
The student will read and perform quarter, half and whole note rhythms accurately. (NS 5A)

- Rhythm reading drills using quarter, half, whole notes.

POSTURE/BREATH/TONE

Posture: A good singing posture helps produce good breathing for singing. An effective singing posture includes the following:

• Stand with feet apart
• Knees unlocked
• Back straight
• Head erect
• Rib cage lifted
• Shoulders relaxed
• Hands at your side

Standing posture   Raising the rib cage

1. To help develop good posture for singing, practice this exercise: Place your fingertips on the crown of your head (elbows out). Notice how your rib cage is raised. Slowly open your arms and continue in a downward arc until they rest at your sides. Try to maintain the raised rib cage as you lower your arms.

Breath: An expanded rib cage increases breath capacity and provides the basis for a free, relaxed and pleasing vocal tone. The following exercise will help you expand the rib cage and take a full breath for singing.

2. Raise your arms overhead slowly while inhaling, then exhale your air on a "ss" while slowly lowering your arms to their original position. Try to maintain the raised rib cage while lowering your arms.

Tone: While you use your voice everyday for communication, singing requires a different way of producing a sound. A "yawn-sigh" is a very useful exercise that helps prepare the voice to produce a full, relaxed, free and pleasing tone.

3. Yawn-sigh — Yawn, then starting on a high pitch, produce a relaxed descending vocal sigh on an "ah" vowel, somewhat like a siren.

"Singers will slump! Expect to continually reinforce the steps to good posture."

TEACHING SUGGESTIONS

Essential Elements:
The student will develop the posture and breath control needed to support choral tone. (NS 1A)

Focus:
Good posture helps produce good breathing which leads to good vocal tone.

Teaching Tips:
• Teacher models good posture, identifying the 7 steps to good posture.
• Students rehearse good posture.
• Check student posture often throughout rehearsal.
• Perform breathing exercise with students. Ask students to turn or move apart slightly so that they have room to raise their arms.
• Ask students to notice the feeling the expanded rib cage produces.
• Perform the exercise several times, increasing the length of exhalation each time.
• Repeat breathing exercise with arms at side, keeping the same expanded rib cage feeling.

• The yawn-sigh will help young singers find their head voice and also serve as a relaxation tool. Use it frequently throughout rehearsal.
• Keep the classroom atmosphere light and relaxed while performing the yawn-sigh, and move quickly to the next activity. One or two yawn-sighs are usually sufficient.
• Spend very little rehearsal time on this page, but encourage students frequently throughout the rehearsal to demonstrate good posture, breath and tone.

RHYTHM

Rhythm is the organization of sound length (duration).

Beat is a steadily recurring pulse.

Rhythm Practice:
Practice keeping a steady beat as a group. Clap, tap, or chant with a clock or metronome.

Note values: Three common note values are the *quarter* note, the *half* note, and the *whole* note.

Quarter note   Half note   Whole note

In most of the music that we'll begin with, the quarter note will be assigned the beat.

You'll notice from the chart below that *two quarter notes* have the same duration as *one half note*, and that *two half notes* (or four quarters) have the same duration as *one whole note*.

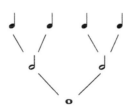

Check Your Knowledge!

1. What is *rhythm*?

2. What is a *beat*?

3. Identify the following notes:

4. How many quarter notes equal the same duration as a half note?

5. How many half notes equal the same duration as a whole note?

6. How many quarter notes equal the same duration as a whole note?

TEACHING SUGGESTIONS

Essential Elements:
The student will understand beat and rhythm, and be able to read and perform quarter, half and whole notes accurately. (NS 5A, 5C, 5D)

Focus:
Maintaining a steady beat is at the heart of musical performance.

Teaching Tips:
• *Ask students to practice keeping the steady beat by clapping, tapping or chanting as a group.*
• *Tap the steady beat as a group to a recording of rhythmic music.*
• *Encourage students to tap softly (tap gently against their side; tap into the air like shaking an imaginary maraca; silently tap fingers on desk or palm of other hand). Clapping is often too intrusive while singing or counting aloud.*
• *Introduce quarter, half and whole notes. (Choose a counting method, and continue using that method throughout this course. See page 189 in the appendix for an overview of common counting methods.)*

• *Practice chanting quarter, half, and whole notes to a steady beat. For example, direct students to tap a steady beat and chant quarter notes, then switch to half notes, then whole notes.*
• *Review the material and answer the questions in Check Your Knowledge! (All answers are located within the text on this page.).*
• *Transfer performance of steady beat to notation by practicing student page 3-4.*

RHYTHM PRACTICE

Identify these note values. Practice aloud by echoing your teacher.

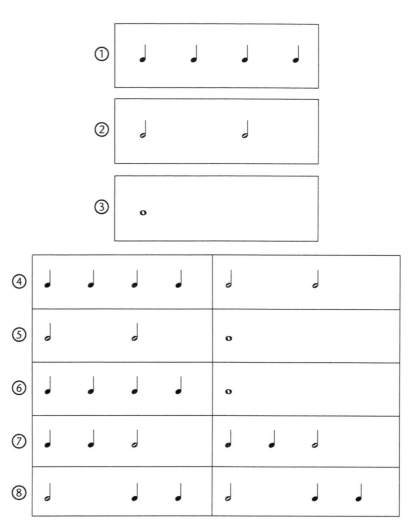

Essential Elements:
- (Extension) The student will compose rhythm patterns of quarter, half, and whole note patterns. (NS 4A)

Teaching Tips: (continued)
- Using your chosen rhythm method, practice these rhythm patterns in an echo-response format.
- For more practice, read lines 1-8 without pausing.

Extension:
- For extra practice, the teacher may create additional patterns of quarter, half and whole notes for the group to read.

RHYTHM PRACTICE

Read each line (clap, tap, or chant). Concentrate on keeping a steady beat. Repeat as necessary until you've mastered the exercise.

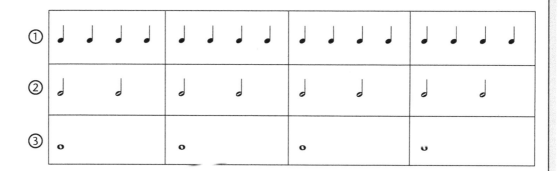

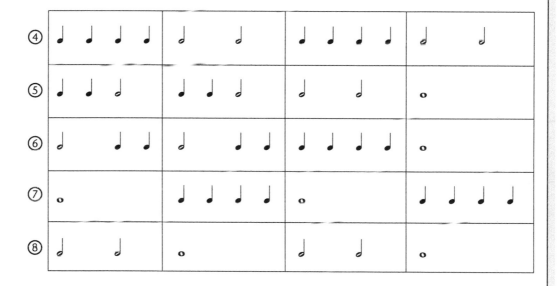

TEACHING SUGGESTIONS

Essential Elements:
The student will read and perform quarter, half and whole note rhythms accurately. (NS 5A)
- (Extension) The student will compose rhythm exercises of quarter, half, and whole note patterns. (NS 4A)

Focus:
The students will become independent readers.

Teaching Tips:
- Read each line separately by chanting in your chosen rhythm reading method while keeping a steady beat.
- Read several lines consecutively.
- Divide the singers into groups, and perform two or more lines simultaneously.

Extension:
- Encourage the students to create and notate their own rhythm exercises using quarter, half and whole notes.
- Perform the compositions in class.

EE2: GOALS AND OVERVIEW

EE2 continues with the basics of vocal production and notation. Integrate the material in this chapter with other beginning-of-the-semester activities such as getting acquainted with your choir members, categorizing their voice types, and choosing beginning choral literature for them to perform.

SPECIAL NOTE: *Essential Repertoire for the Young Choir* (Treble, Tenor Bass and Mixed voicings) includes literature in a variety of styles and periods especially selected for young adolescent voices.

In addition to providing beginning vocal exercises, EE2 provides drill in pitch identification.

ESSENTIAL ELEMENTS AND NEW CONCEPTS

Voice:
The student will develop the posture and breath control needed to support choral tone. (NS 1A)
The student will sing with tall, vertically-shaped uniform vowels. (NS 1A)

• Five basic vowels (ee, eh, ah, oh, oo)
• Vocal exercises using the "ah" vowel

Theory:
The student will become familiar with the grand staff, pitch names, and clefs, as they relate to the piano keyboard. (NS 5C, 5D)

• staff, grand staff
• names of the lines and spaces
• Middle C
• Treble clef, Bass clef
• Pitch identification practice

Sight-Reading:
The student will echo and read melodic patterns. (NS 5B, 5E)

• Echo sing short melodic patterns.

POSTURE/BREATH/TONE

Posture: Review the steps for a good singing posture. Remember that a good posture helps produce good breathing for singing.

- Stand with feet apart
- Knees unlocked
- Back straight
- Head erect
- Rib cage lifted
- Shoulders relaxed
- Hands at your side

Breath: Remember that an expanded rib cage helps develop expanded breath capacity. Practice the following exercises:

1. Raise your arms overhead slowly while inhaling, then exhale your air on a "ss" while slowly lowering your arms to their original position. Try to maintain the raised rib cage while lowering your arms.

2. Repeat Exercises #1, but exhale with 4 short "ss" sounds followed by a longer "ss" sound:

   ss ss ss ss ss_____ (repeat once or twice in one breath)

3. Imagine there is a milkshake as large as the room. Hold your arms out from your body as if you were holding the giant milkshake and "drink" the air through a giant straw. Exhale on a yawn-sigh.

Tone: *Vowels* are the basis for a good choral tone, so make sure that you sing all vowels with a *relaxed jaw*, a *vertical mouth shape*, and with *space inside your mouth*. This helps each singer to produce a full and free vocal tone quality that blends well with other voices to create a pleasing choral sound.

The *five basic vowels* include:

ee

eh

ah

oh

oo

Notice that each vowel sound is produced with a relaxed and vertical dropped jaw.

TEACHING SUGGESTIONS

Essential Elements:
- The student will develop the posture and breath control needed to support choral tone.
  (NS 1A)
- The student will sing with tall, uniform vowels.
  (NS 1A)

Focus:
Tall vowels are a basis for good choral tone.

Teaching Tips:
- *Review the posture procedures and practice the breathing exercises as listed above.*
- *Teacher should demonstrate the mouth position for each of the five basic vowels, emphasizing relaxed jaw and vertical mouth shape with space inside the mouth. Ask students to imitate.*

POSTURE/BREATH/TONE

At this time, we'll focus on the "ah" vowel. Here are several exercises to apply the principle of the *relaxed jaw* and *vertical mouth shape*:

4. Sing the following exercise with a relaxed jaw. Hold the last note and listen to see that you are producing a full, blended choral sound that is in tune with the voices around you. Repeat at different pitch levels both higher and lower, and use the different text syllables as indicated.

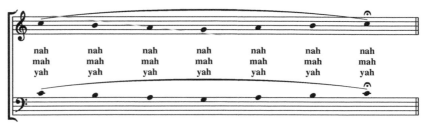

5. Sing the following exercise first with 1 text syllable for each separate note and then 1 text syllable for two notes slurred (connected) together. Repeat at different pitch levels both higher and lower.

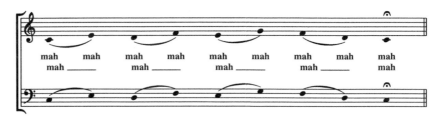

6. Sing "America." Notice how many "ah" vowels appear in the text. NOTE: Some of these vowels are part of a vowel blend (also called a *diphthong*). For example, "my" is really two vowel sounds: ah + ee. Concentrate primarily on the "ah" of this diphthong.
   • Maintain a dropped jaw for all vowels and especially the "ah."
   • Take a full expanded rib cage breath. Can you sing a whole phrase in one breath?

       (ah)(ah)   (ah)   (ah)   (ah) (ah)
(breathe) My country 'tis of thee, sweet land of liberty, of thee I sing.

           (ah)(ah)   (ah)   (ah)   (ah)
(breathe) Land where my fathers died, Land of the pilgrims' pride,

      (ah)   (ah) (ah)   (ah)
(breathe) From ev'ry mountainside, let freedom ring.

> "The quest for tall vowels is a lifelong journey!"

Teaching Tips: *(continued)*

• *Practice the exercises on this page.*
• *One way to avoid a horizontal mouth position is to hold finger tips gently on both sides of the mouth while singing. This reminds the students to keep a vertical mouth shape.*

Extension:
• *Encourage students to mark all the "ah" vowels in music they are currently rehearsing.*
• *Evaluate students' mastery of tall vowels by videotaping the singers performing the exercises on this page.*

BASIC NOTATION

A *staff* is a graph of 5 lines and 4 spaces on which music is written. The staff shown below is a *grand staff*. A grand staff is a grouping of two staves.

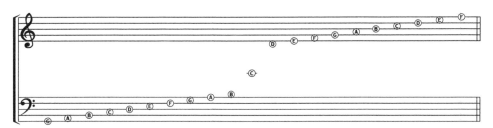

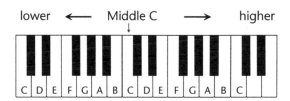

Notice the two symbols at the beginning of the staves on the left hand side. These are called clefs. A *clef* is a symbol that identifies a set of pitches. The *Treble Clef* generally refers to pitches higher than middle C. The *Bass Clef* generally refers to pitches lower than middle C. Notice that middle C has its own little line and may be written in either clef – either at the bottom of the treble clef or the top of the bass clef.

Treble Clef (G Clef)
Second line is G
(The curve of the Clef
loops around the G line.)

Bass Clef (F Clef)
Fourth line is F
(The dots of the clef surround
the F line.)

An easy way to learn the notes on the treble clef staff is to remember that the spaces spell the word *FACE* from the bottom up. An easy way to learn the notes on the bass clef staff is to remember that the spaces spell *ACEG* or *All Cows Eat Grass*. Make up your own phrase for the acronym *GBDFA* (for the bass clef lines) and *EGBDF* (for the treble clef lines).

TEACHING SUGGESTIONS

Essential Elements:
• The student will become familiar with the grand staff, pitch names, and clefs, as they relate to the piano keyboard. (NS 5C, 5D)

Focus:
Pitch notation is basic to music reading.

Teaching Tips:
• Read and discuss the material on this page, demonstrating at the keyboard, working on the computer, illustrating with various pitched classroom instruments, etc.
• Emphasize the importance of learning the pitch names.
• Quick recognition of pitch names is necessary, so practice and drill is important.

Check your knowledge!

1. What is the name of the graph of lines and spaces on which music is written?

2. How many lines and spaces does this graph have?

3. What is the name of the symbol used to describe a set of pitches? Name two types of these symbols.

4. Give another name for *G Clef*. Give another name for *F Clef*.

5. Name the pitch which may be written on its own little line in either clef.

Practice

Name the notes in the following examples.

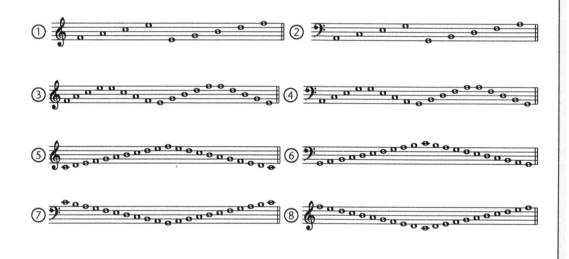

Teaching Tips: (continued)

• Complete the **Check Your Knowledge!** section to check for understanding. All answers are included within the text on student p. 7.
• Practice naming the notes in cooperative learning groups or large groups. Flash cards may be helpful. Avoid tedious drill by varying the activities.

PRACTICE—NOTE IDENTIFICATION

Practice echo-singing these notes by letter name.

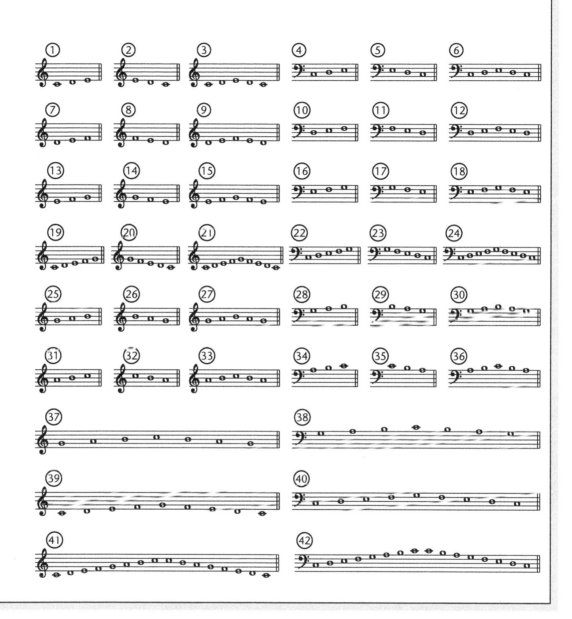

TEACHING SUGGESTIONS

Essential Elements:
• The student will echo and read melodic patterns.
  (NS 5B, 5E)

Focus:
The student will begin to connect sound with
  symbol.

Teaching Tips:
• Echo-sing this page quickly to increase pitch
  reading facility.
• All students should sing all exercises in an
  appropriate octave.
• Encourage changing voices to switch octaves as
  necessary. Changing voices may need to omit
  certain notes in exercises 41 and 42.
• Teachers should be patient and understanding
  with new baritones who may be unable to sing
  exercise 34-38. Encourage them to use a light,
  unforced tone on the high notes.

EE3: GOALS AND OVERVIEW

In this chapter, the students will be introduced to the concept of *diaphragmatic* breathing, along with increasing their repertoire of vocalises. Teachers are encouraged to apply and adapt these exercises to repertoire being rehearsed. Remember that students of this level of age and experience need repetition of a particular vocalise until it is mastered. Applying the concept to new situations likewise requires practice and repetition.

Also in this chapter, students will continue to expand their knowledge of notation, now including short melodies to echo-sing and read. The chapter expands to include *PERFORMANCE*, in this case a short speech chorus which combines rhythm with text.

ESSENTIAL ELEMENTS AND NEW CONCEPTS

Voice:
The student will develop the posture and diaphragmatic breathing needed to support choral tone. (NS 1A)
The student will sing tall uniform "oo" vowels. (NS 1A)

- Activating the diaphragm
- Vocal exercises using the "oo" vowel

Theory:
The students will understand the concepts of measure, barline, and meter. (NS 5D)
(Extension) The student will compose rhythm exercises of quarter, half, and whole note patterns. (NS 4A)

- Measure, barline, double barline
- Meter, time signature
- $\frac{4}{4}$, $\frac{3}{4}$, $\frac{2}{4}$

Sight-Reading:
The student will read and perform rhythm patterns in various meters. (NS 5A)
The student will echo-sing rhythmic pitch patterns. (NS 5A, 5B, 5E)

- Read rhythm patterns in $\frac{4}{4}$, $\frac{3}{4}$, $\frac{2}{4}$
- Echo-sing and read short unison melodies

Performance:
The student will be introduced to classical period instruments. (NS 6B, 6C, 9B)
The student will become familiar with musical terms presented on this page. (NS 5C)
The student will read a speech chorus which combines text and rhythm. (NS 1E)

- Music History – the development of the piano
- Musical terms – piano, forte
- Unison speech chorus combining text and rhythm

Practice voice-builders everyday

POSTURE/BREATH

Posture: Review the steps to a good singing posture.

- Stand with feet apart
- Knees unlocked
- Back straight
- Head erect
- Rib cage lifted
- Shoulders relaxed
- Hands at your side

Breath: Remember that a lifted and expanded rib cage helps to develop expanded breath capacity. When you sing a musical phrase supported by a good singing breath, you are demonstrating good breath support.

1. Bend at the waist and pick an imaginary flower. Inhale the "fragrance" while slowly standing up. Exhale on a yawn-sigh.

Diaphragmatic Breathing: One aspect of breath support is the lifted and expanded rib cage. Another aspect of breath support is the process of activating the *diaphragm*. The diaphragm is a muscle just below the lungs that moves downward during inhalation as the rib cage expands and air fills the lungs. Exercises which help you become aware of this action of the diaphragm can help you learn to energize and enrich the vocal sound you are producing.

2. When people are surprised or frightened, they usually take in a rapid breath with a notice-able movement of the diaphragm. Place your hand just below your rib cage and above your waist and then take a "surprised breath."
   - Do you feel the movement?
   - Did your hand move as a result of the surprised breath?

3. See if you can produce the same movement of the diaphragm as in #2 in the following exercise. Use short *whispered* sounds, no voice.

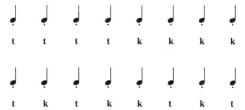

TEACHING SUGGESTIONS

Essential Elements:
- The student will develop the posture and diaphragmatic breathing needed to support choral tone. (NS 1A)
- The student will sing tall, uniform "oo" vowels. (NS 1A)
- (Extension) The student will apply information learned in music (anatomy of the breathing mechanism) to science class. (NS 8B)

Focus:
- Diaphragmatic breathing is the foundation of good singing.

Teaching Tips:
- Practice the exercises on this page.
- For more detailed information about the physiology of the diaphragm see the illustration on p. 80.

Extension:
- Borrow models or charts of the human breathing mechanism from your science teacher to illustrate this physiology more completely.

BREATH/TONE

4. Practice the following exercise, keeping the sounds short and detached. Use the diaphragm as in #3 to support and energize the tone. Repeat at different pitch levels, both higher and lower:

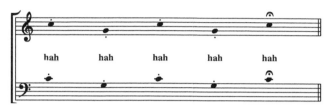

5. Do the exercise above, but this time use an "oo" vowel. Remember to keep a relaxed jaw, vertical mouth position, and space inside the mouth.
   - Keep the sounds short and detached.
   - Support the tone by activating the diaphragm.

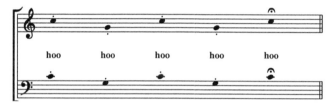

6. In the following exercise, sing the musical pitches so they are smooth and connected.
   - Take a full expanded rib cage breath supported by the action of the diaphragm (even though in this exercise the notes are connected and not short).
   - Sing the "oo" vowel with rounded lips, a relaxed jaw, and vertical space inside the mouth.
   - Repeat at different pitch levels, both higher and lower.

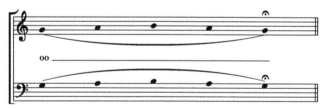

Teaching Tips: (continued)

- *Review the "ah" vowel by performing exercise 4. Check for vertical mouth positon.*
- *The "oo" vowel requires space in the mouth. To experience the space, sing a tall "ah" vowel and gradually round the lips to an "oo," maintaining the vertical space in the mouth.*
- *Rehearse the "oo" vowel exercises on this page.*
- *Repeat exercises at different pitch levels to accomodate differing voice ranges.*

MEASURES • METERS • BARLINES

Barlines are vertical lines that divide the staff into smaller sections called measures. A *double barline* indicates the end of a section or piece of music.

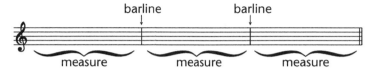

Meter is a form of rhythmic organization. For example:

4 = Four beats per measure (♩ ♩ ♩ ♩)
4 = The quarter note (♩) receives the beat

3 = Three beats per measure (♩ ♩ ♩)
4 = The quarter note (♩) receives the beat

2 = Two beats per measure (♩ ♩)
4 – The quarter note (♩) receives the beat

The numbers that identify the meter are called the *time signature*. The time signature is placed after the clef at the beginning of a song or section of a song.

Check your knowledge!
1. What are the vertical lines that divide a staff into smaller sections called?

2. Name the smaller divided sections of a staff.

3. What is a *double barline*?

4. Describe *meter*.

5. What are the numbers that identify the meter called?

6. Describe the following meters:

TEACHING SUGGESTIONS

Essential Elements:
• The students will understand the concepts of measure, barline, and meter. (NS 5D)
• (Extension) The student will compose rhythm patterns of quarter, half, and whole note patterns. (NS 4A)

Focus:
Meter is a form of rhythmic organization.

Teaching Tips:
• *Read and discuss the information on this page.*
• *Review the material and answer the questions in Check Your Knowledge! (All answers are located in the text on this page.)*

Higher Level Thinking:
• *Encourage students to create a four-measure rhythm composition using quarter, half, and whole notes in ²₄, ³₄ or ⁴₄ meter.*
• *Ask students to perform these compositions for the class on rhythm instruments of their choice.*

RHYTHM PRACTICE

Clap, tap, or chant.

①

②

③

④

⑤

⑥

⑦

⑧

⑨

TEACHING SUGGESTIONS

Essential Elements:
- The student will read and perform rhythm patterns in various meters. (NS 5A)
- The student will echo-sing rhythmic pitch patterns. (NS 5A, 5B, 5E)

Focus:
- Putting it all together: rhythm, meter, and pitch.

Teaching Tips:
- Perform exercises 1-9 using your chosen method of rhythm reading.

Extension:
- Introduce students to the conducting patterns for $\frac{4}{4}$, $\frac{3}{4}$, and $\frac{2}{4}$.
- Ask students to conduct and read exercises 1-9.

PITCH REVIEW

Echo sing or sing as a group.

Teaching Tips: *(continued)*

- *On this page students echo-sing short melodies which include both pitch, rhythm and meter for the first time.*
- *Echo-sing each exercise, maintaining the steady beat.*
- *Encourage students to keep the steady beat by tapping softly as they sing.*
- *Encourage changing voices to switch octaves as necessary. Changing voices may need to omit certain notes in exercises 3 or 5.*
- *Strive to maintain a good choral tone.*

MUSICAL TERMS

History: The piano, a stringed instrument whose strings are struck by hammers activated by keys, was developed in the 18th century and originally called the pianoforte, an Italian term meaning "soft-loud." It was called this because unlike an earlier keyboard instrument called the harpsichord, the loudness of the piano's sound could be varied by the touch of the fingers.

Musical Terms

p - piano; soft

f - forte; loud

Apply what you've learned about music reading to this short speech chorus.
- After you sight-read the rhythm, repeat with the printed text.
- Repeat as necessary for accuracy.

The Months Of The Year

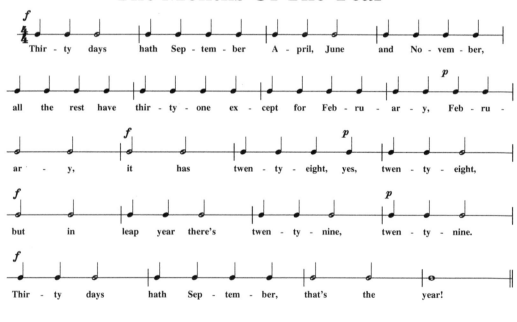

TEACHING SUGGESTIONS

Essential Elements:
- The student will be introduced to Classical period instruments. (NS 6B, 6C, 9B)
- The student will become familiar with musical terms presented on this page. (NS 5C)
- The student will combine text and rhythm. (NS 1E)

Focus:
Dynamics add interest to music.

Teaching Tips:
- Read the information about the piano. Relate that information to the dynamic terms listed.
- Sight-read the speech chorus following the sequence suggested above.
- Rehearse again, emphasizing dynamics.

Extension:
- Perform "The Months of the Year" in canon with two or more groups entering one measure apart.

EE4: GOALS AND OVERVIEW

EE4 is the first of a series of review and practice chapters. This gives the students and teacher a chance to evaluate the prior learning and determine if more practice or re-teaching is necessary. The material varies from specific knowledge-based questions to musical exercises for drill and practice and higher-level thinking skills of choral performance.

Teachers are encouraged to use group discussion to cover knowledge-based review questions. This useful activity allows you to identify student misunderstandings of the material, and provides you with a forum for re-teaching the material. In some cases the questions are rephrased slightly to allow you to assess students' higher-level thinking skills.

The musical examples for sight-reading and performance allow you to assess the students' mastery of the particular musical concepts that have been presented in previous chapters. If the students have clearly mastered the material, it is not necessary to perform all the sight-reading exercises. If, however, they need more practice, these drills and short songs give you an opportunity to "set" the learning before additional new concepts are presented in subsequent chapters.

ESSENTIAL ELEMENTS AND NEW CONCEPTS

Voice:
The student will describe and demonstrate the posture, breathing, and vowel placement necessary for good singing tone. (NS 1A)

• Review Chapters 1-3

Theory:
The student will describe and review elements of musical notation. (NS 5C, 5D)

• Review Chapters 1-3

Sight-Reading:
The student will read and sing rhythmic and melodic patterns. (NS 5A, 5B, 5C)

• Read rhythm patterns using quarter, half, whole notes in $\frac{2}{4}$, $\frac{3}{4}$ and $\frac{4}{4}$ meter
• Identify notes on the staff
• Read or echo-sing stepwise melodies

Performance:
The student will become familiar with the musical terms presented on this page. (NS 5C)
The student will combine text and rhythm. (NS 1F)
(Extension) The student will compose a rhythmic setting of a tongue twister and arrange it for voices and classroom instruments. (NS 4A)
(Extension) The student will compose original lyrics and arrange them for voices and classroom instruments. (NS 8B)

• Musical terms: crescendo
• Unison speech chorus combining text and rhythm

REVIEW/PRACTICE

In group discussion, answer the following questions, giving examples or illustrating where possible. Refer to VOICE-BUILDERS in Chapters 1-3 as needed.

1. Describe the steps to a good singing posture.

2. How does good posture affect singing?

3. How does an expanded rib cage affect breathing?

4. What is a yawn-sigh?

5. List the five basic vowels.

6. Describe three things you should do to produce the basic mouth position in singing the five basic vowels.

7. What is the basic vowel sound in the word "from." Describe or illustrate the basic mouth position for singing this vowel.

8. Describe two aspects of breath support.

9. What is the muscle called that is below the lungs and that moves downward during inhalation?

10. What is the basic vowel sound in the word "who." Describe or illustrate the basic mouth position for singing this vowel.

History: The development of a simple and melodious vocal style of singing during the 17th century was called *bel canto*, from the Italian meaning "beautiful singing." Later, bel canto became associated not only with beauty of sound, but also with brilliant performance, especially in the operas of Mozart and Italian composers of the 18th century. One famous Mozart opera is *The Magic Flute*.

TEACHING SUGGESTIONS

Essential Elements:
• The student will describe and demonstrate the posture, breathing, and vowel placement necessary for good singing tone. (NS 1A)

Focus:
Review information learned in Chapters 1-3.

Teaching Tips:
• Answer the questions on this page orally either in large group or a cooperative learning situation.

Answers: *(page numbers refer to the student text)*
1. *Stand with feet apart, knees unlocked, back straight, head erect, rib cage lifted, shoulders relaxed, hands at side (p. 1)*
2. *Good posture helps produce good breathing. (p. 1)*
3. *It increases breath capacity and provides the basis for a free, relaxed and pleasing vocal tone. (p. 1)*
4. *A yawn-sigh is a relaxed, descending vocal sigh on an "ah" vowel. (p. 1)*
5. *The five basic vowels are ee, eh, ah, oh, oo. (p. 5)*
6. *A relaxed jaw, a vertical mouth shape, space inside the mouth. (p. 5)*
7. *"Ah" is the basic vowel in "from." An "ah" vowel has a relaxed jaw and vertical mouth shape. (p. 6)*

8. *Breath support includes a lifted and expanded rib cage and an activated diaphragm. (p. 10)*
9. *Diaphragm (p. 10)*
10. *"Oo" is the basic vowel in "who." To sing an "oo" use rounded lips, a relaxed jaw and vertical space inside the mouth. (p. 11)*

Extension:
• *Discuss beautiful singing throughout history. See the **History** segment on this page.*
• *Listen to a recording of bel canto singing (perhaps the "**Queen of the Night**" aria from **The Magic Flute**.)*

THEORY BUILDERS 4

REVIEW/PRACTICE

In group discussion, answer the following questions, giving examples or illustrating where possible. Refer to THEORY-BUILDERS in Chapters 1-3 as needed.

1. What is *rhythm*?

2. What is a steadily recurring pulse called?

3. Identify the following notes.

4. How many quarter notes equal a whole note? How many half notes equal a whole note?

5. How many lines are in a staff? How many spaces are in a staff?

6. What is a *clef*? Name two types of clefs.

7. Which clef is middle C written in?

8. What are *barlines*? What is a *double barline*?

9. Name a form of rhythmic organization.

10. What is a *time signature*? Name and describe three time signatures.

Matching

① 𝄢   a) quarter notes

② 𝄞   b) middle C

③ ♩ ♩ ♩ ♩   c) bass clef

④ 𝅝   d) treble clef

⑤ 𝅗𝅥 𝅗𝅥   e) half notes

⑥   f) time signature

⑦ 𝄴   g) whole note

TEACHING SUGGESTIONS

Essential Elements:
• The student will describe and review elements of musical notation. (NS 5C, 5D)

Focus:
Review information learned in Chapters 1-3.

Teaching Tips
• Answer the questions on this page orally either in large group or a cooperative learning situation.

Answers: (page numbers refer to the student text)
1. Rhythm is organization of sound length (duration). (p. 2)
2. Beat is a steadily recurring pulse. (p. 2)
3. Quarter note, half note, whole note. (p. 2)
4. Four quarter notes = a whole note. Two half notes = a whole note. (p. 2)
5. Five lines are in a staff. Four spaces are in a staff (p. 7)

6. A clef is a symbol that identifies a set of pitches. Two types are treble and bass. (p. 7)
7. Middle C can be written in either clef. (p. 7)
8. Barlines are vertical lines that divide the staff into smaller sections. A double barline indicates the end of a section or piece of music. (p. 12)
9. A form of rhythmic organization is meter. (p. 12)
10. A time signature is the numbers that identify the meter. $\frac{2}{4}$, $\frac{3}{4}$, $\frac{4}{4}$ (p. 12)

Matching:
1=C, 2=D, 3=A, 4=G, 5=E, 6=B, 7=F

RHYTHM PRACTICE

Clap, tap, or chant.

①

②

③

④

⑤

⑥

⑦

⑧

TEACHING SUGGESTIONS

Essential Elements:
• The students will read and sing rhythmic and melodic patterns. (NS 5A, 5B, 5C)

Focus:
Apply sight-reading information learned in Chapters 1-3.

Teaching Tips:
• Encourage students to keep the steady beat throughout these exercises and whenever sight-reading.
• Use your chosen method of reading rhythm. (See the appendix on pg. 189.)

Student Book Page **19**

PITCH PRACTICE

Speak the following pitches, echo sing or sing as a group.

"Lots of practice equals fluency. Repetition and practice of new material is necessary, but don't get bogged down on any single exercise."

Teaching Tips: (continued)

- Echo-sing the exercises 1-7 on student page 19-20,

OR

- If the group is ready, sight-read the exercises using the following sequence:
1. Speak the rhythm using your chosen method.
2. Speak the pitches in rhythm using your chosen method.
3. Sing the pitches in rhythm.

- Encourage changing voices to switch octaves as necessary.
- Changing voices may need to omit selected pitches or change octaves in exercises 3-5.
- Teachers should be patient and understanding of new baritones who may be unable to sing portions of exercises 2-5.

MORE PITCH PRACTICE

Name the following pitches, echo sing or sing as a group.

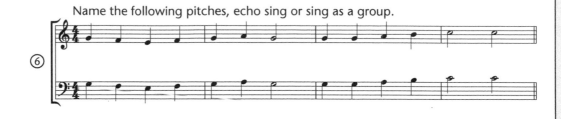

⑥

⑦

Name these pitches as above. Notice the more extreme range.

⑧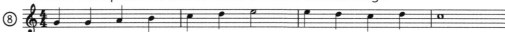

⑨

Teaching Tips: (continued)

• *Review the pitches in the more extreme range as presented in exercises 8-9. Some voices may be able to demonstrate these pitches.*

MUSICAL TERMS

Musical terms
cresc. — crescendo; an Italian word which means gradually louder.

Apply what you've learned about music reading to this short speech chorus.
* Sight-read the rhythm, and repeat as needed to become accurate.
* Repeat with the printed text.

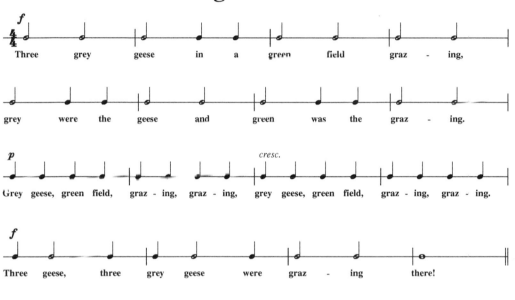

Tongue Twister

TEACHING SUGGESTIONS

Essential Elements:
* The student will become familiar with musical terms presented on this page. (NS 5C)
* The student will combine text and rhythm. (NS 1E)

Focus:
The crescendo adds interest to music.

Teaching Tips:
* Present the lesson as described above.

Extension:
* After students can perform "Tongue Twister" successfully, perform it as a canon with two or more groups entering one measure apart.

Higher Level Thinking:
* Encourage students to create original rhythmic settings of familiar tongue twisters.
* Some students may want to create their own lyrics, poems, texts or tongue twisters.

* (Extension) The student will compose a rhythmic setting of a tongue twister and arrange it for voices and classroom instruments. (NS 4A)
* (Extension) The student will compose original lyrics and arrange them for voices and classroom instruments. (NS 8B)

EE5: GOALS AND OVERVIEW

This chapter takes the concept of pitch and extends it into the concept of tonality. The importance of key, keynote, and scale in the process of sight-reading cannot be overemphasized.

If you have not yet chosen a sight-reading method, this is a good time to do so. By using a method consistently and systematically, young singers should find it easier to connect the sound with the symbol. Several methods are described in the appendix on page 186.

Remember, however, to continue to stress the steady beat and accuracy in rhythm. Often when singers stumble over a melodic pattern, it is the rhythm, rather than the pitch that has caused the error. A good policy, especially with younger or less-experienced choirs is to always chant the rhythm before adding pitch.

An important part of this method is the inclusion of actual songs, which allow the choir to apply the concepts they have been studying to the performance of "real music." "Rain" uses only stepwise, unison melodies, and rhythms consisting of only quarter, half, and whole notes, but nonetheless provides a real feeling of satisfaction and accomplishment.

ESSENTIAL ELEMENTS AND NEW CONCEPTS

Voice:
The student will develop the posture and breath control needed to support choral tone. (NS 1A)

- The "oh" vowel

Theory:
The student will identify and describe the concepts of pitch, scale, and key. (NS 5C, 5D)

(Extension) The student will apply language arts skills during music class by listing different words which mean *pitch*. (NS 8B)

- Pitch, scale, key, keynote
- Key of C

Sight-Reading:
The student will echo and read melodic patterns in the key of C. (NS 5A, 5B, 5D, 5E)

(Extension) The student will describe the polyphonic entrances of soprano, alto, tenor and bass voices using appropriate musical terminology. (NS 6A)

- Practice with melodic patterns in the key of C
- The four voice types: soprano, alto, tenor, bass
- Combinable exercises (harmony)

Performance:
The student will apply music reading skills to the performance of short a cappella songs. (NS 5E)

The student will apply music reading skills to the performance of a short accompanied song. (NS 5E)

(Extension) The student will improvise short melodies in the key of C over repeated rhythm patterns. (NS 3C)

- 3 short unison songs in C major
- Accompanied unison song, "Rain"

POSTURE/BREATH/TONE

Posture: Review the steps to a good singing posture.
- Stand with feet apart
- Knees unlocked
- Back straight
- Head erect
- Rib cage lifted
- Shoulders relaxed
- Hands at your side

Breath: Put your hands on the sides of your rib cage and inhale. Notice the movement of the rib cage. Breathe out on a whispered "ah."

Tone: The following exercises focus on the "oh" vowel. Notice in the illustration that the lips are more rounded than the "ah" vowel, but more open than the "oo" vowel. Remember to keep vertical space inside your mouth as you sing all these vowels:

ah   oh   oo

1. As you sing this exercise remember to:
   - Keep the sounds short and detached.
   - Support the tone by activating the diaphragm.
   - Repeat at different pitch levels, both higher and lower.

hah	hah	hah	hah	hah
hoo	hoo	hoo	hoo	hoo
hoh	hoh	hoh	hoh	hoh

TEACHING SUGGESTIONS

Essential Elements:
- The student will develop the posture and breath control needed to support choral tone. (NS 1A)

Focus:
"Oh" vowels sung with rounded lips and vertical space in the mouth lead to beautiful singing.

Teaching Tips:
- Remind singers about the importance of good posture and breathing.
- Perform the exercises as described on student pages 22-23.

TONE

2. In the following exercise, sing the musical pitches so they are smooth and connected.
   • Take a full supported rib cage breath.
   • Sing the "oh" vowel with rounded lips and vertical space inside the mouth.
   • Sing the pitches so they are smooth and connected.

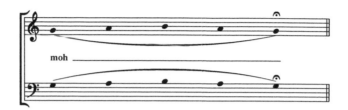

moh

3. In the following exercise, connect two notes together on the syllable "moh." Be sure that your mouth doesn't change shape to an "oo" as you prepare to sing the consonant "m."

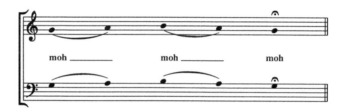

moh _____ moh _____ moh

4. In the following exercise, each word uses an "oh" vowel.

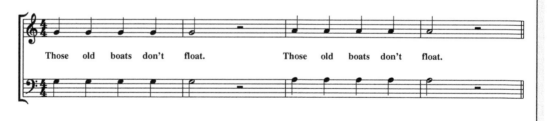

Those old boats don't float.   Those old boats don't float.

Teaching Tips: *(continued)*

• *Ask students to find and circle "oh" vowels in the music they are performing.*

Extension:
• *Encourage (and expect) the students to apply what they have learned about the "oh" vowel at all times in the music they perform. Give them continual reinforcement.*

Student Book Page 24

PITCH • SCALE • KEY OF C

Pitch — the highness or lowness of musical sound.

Scale — an inventory or collection of pitches. The word "scale" (from the Italian *scala*) means ladder. Thus, many musical scales are a succession of pitches higher and lower.

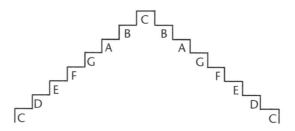

Key — The importance of one pitch over the others in a scale. Frequently, the key note or tone might be described as the home tone. In the Key of C, C is the home tone or keynote.

Key of C Scale

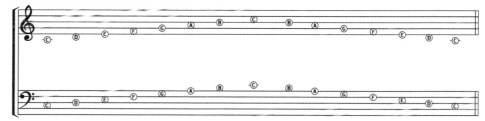

"*This is a good point to introduce the method you have chosen for sight-reading pitch. There are a number of effective sight-reading methods described on page 186. They include movable Do, fixed Do, and numbers. Use one of these methods consistently throughout this course.*"

Check your knowledge!

1. What is *pitch*?

2. Define *scale*. Define *scala*.

3. Describe *key*. Describe *keynote*.

TEACHING SUGGESTIONS

Essential Elements:
• The student will define pitch, scale and key. (NS 5C, 5D)
• (Extension) The student will apply language arts skills by listing different words which mean **pitch**. (NS 8B)

Focus:
C is the home tone or keynote in the key (or scale) of C.

Teaching Tips:
• Prior to this lesson, students have used the term "pitch," and have sung different pitches, but this lesson defines the term.
• Read and orally discuss the material on this page.
• Demonstrate on the keyboard as needed.
• The answers to Check Your Knowledge! are located within the text on this page.

Extension:
• Ask students to notate a C scale on music manuscript paper.

Higher Level Thinking:
• List some different words which mean pitch. (notes, solfege, numbers, letter names, etc.)

KEY OF C PRACTICE

Identify the following pitches in the key of C. Echo-sing these drills with your teacher.

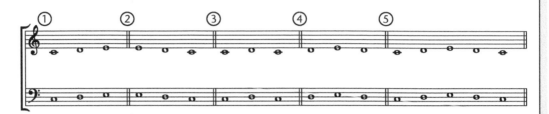

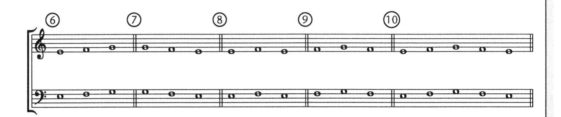

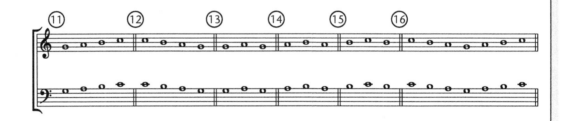

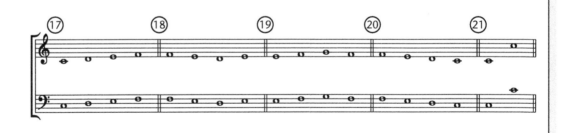

TEACHING SUGGESTIONS

Essential Elements:
• The student will echo and read melodic patterns in the key of C. (NS 5B, 5C, 5D, 5E)

Focus:
The student will practice connecting sound with symbol.

Teaching Tips:
• Echo-sing these patterns using your chosen pitch-reading method.
• All students should sing all exercises in an appropriate octave.
• Encourage changing voices to switch octaves as necessary.
• Teachers should be patient and understanding with new baritones. Encourage them to use a light, unforced tone on the high notes.

RHYTHM AND PITCH

History: Human voices are generally divided into four basic ranges:
soprano — the highest treble voice, usually written in treble clef
alto — a treble voice that is lower than the soprano, usually written in treble clef
tenor — a male voice written in bass clef or treble clef, that is higher than a bass voice
bass — a male voice written in bass clef that is lower than a tenor voice

The following exercises combine pitch and rhythm. Chant the rhythm first, then add the pitches. Repeat as necessary to master each drill.

①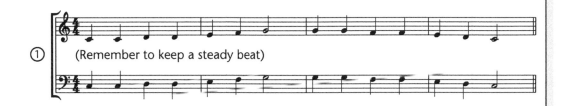

(Remember to keep a steady beat)

②

③

"When students are learning to read music, an established sequence is essential. Follow the sequence below on all subsequent exercises."

Essential Elements:
- (Extension) The student will describe the polyphonic entrances of soprano, alto, tenor and bass voices using appropriate musical terminology. (NS 6A)

Teaching Tips: (continued)
- Read and discuss the information on this page about soprano, alto, tenor and bass voices.
- This may be the students' first real introduction to sight-reading without echo-singing first.
- Ask all students to sing the treble clef exercise 1. Then ask all students to sing the bass clef exercise 1. Lead them to discover that both lines are the same an octave apart.

- Encourage changing voices to switch octaves as necessary.
- Teachers should be patient and understanding with new baritones. Encourage them to use a light, unforced tone on the high notes.

Sight-reading Sequence:
1. Chant the rhythm using your chosen method of rhythm reading.
2. Chant the pitch names in rhythm using your chosen method of pitch reading.
3. Sing the pitches in rhythm using your chosen method of pitch reading.

Extension:
To further reinforce the differences in sound between soprano, alto, tenor and bass voices, play a recording of *"For Unto Us a Child is Born"* from Handel's Messiah. Point out the entrances of each voice part in the opening section.

Student Book Page 27

MELODY • HARMONY

The following exercises combine pitch and rhythm. Chant the rhythm first, then add pitch. Repeat as necessary. When you've mastered all the exercises, you may sing the lines in any combination. For example, divide into two groups with one group singing #1 and the other group singing #2.

Each line sung by itself produces *melody* (a succession of musical tones). When two or more melodies are combined, the result is *harmony* (musical tones sounded simultaneously).

"Combining exercises allows you enough variety to continue practicing a particular concept until it is internalized."

Teaching Tips: *(continued)*

• *These exercises are the student's first introduction to melody and harmony. Note that any line may be combined (sung simultaneously) with any other exercise on this page.*

• *Caution: do not combine lines before the singers are ready. Here is a sequential procedure for sight-reading these exercises and other similar combinable exercise pages in this course:*

1. *Chant rhythm of each line.*
2. *Chant pitch names in rhythm using your chosen pitch-reading method.*
3. *Sing pitches in rhythm.*
4. *Students sing one line while teacher sings a different line.*
5. *Divide class into two (or more) sections and sing two lines.*

Apply what you've learned about music reading to these short songs.
- Chant the rhythm.
- Add pitch. Repeat as necessary for accuracy.
- Sing with text and expression.

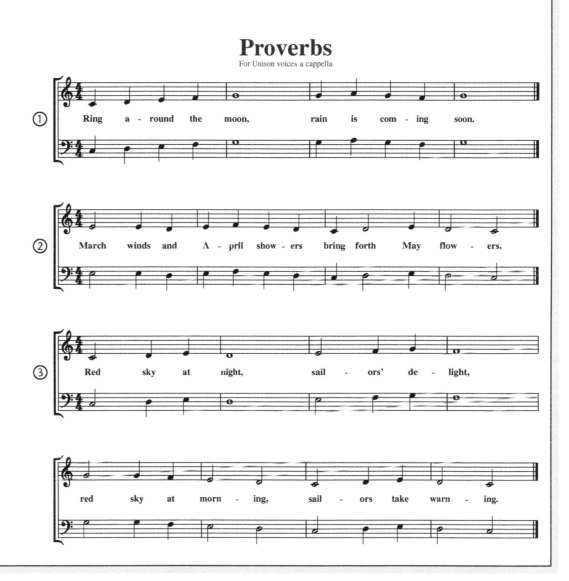

Proverbs
For Unison voices a cappella

① Ring a - round the moon, rain is com - ing soon.

② March winds and A - pril show - ers bring forth May flow - ers.

③ Red sky at night, sail - ors' de - light,

red sky at morn - ing, sail - ors take warn - ing.

TEACHING SUGGESTIONS

Essential Elements:
- The student will apply music reading skills to the performance of short a cappella songs. (NS 5A, 5B, 5E)
- (Extension) The student will improvise short melodies over repeated rhythm patterns. (NS 3C)

Focus:
Transfer reading skills to a song.

Teaching Tips:
- Follow the suggested teaching sequence above.
- Remind singers to use tall, round vowels.

Extension:
Encourage students to improvise or compose short melodies in the key of C using the first five tones in the C scale. Students may want to add their own texts. Orff classroom instruments or keyboards are especially helpful for this assignment. Accompany these melodies with percussion instruments playing a repeated pattern.

Student Book Page **29**

UNISON VOICES

For extra challenge, here is a short song with piano accompaniment.
- Notice the piano part. The piece begins with 4 measures of piano accompaniment.
- Identify the vocal lines. In this piece, the vocal lines are indicated by arrows: →
- Sight-read the rhythm, then speak the pitch names.
- Sing the pitches and repeat as needed to become accurate.
- Add the printed text, then add the piano accompaniment. The voices enter on a C. Practice until you can enter on the correct note.
- Take full expanded rib cage breaths. Sing with expression!

Follow Me
For Unison voices and Piano

Words and Music by
EMILY CROCKER

TEACHING SUGGESTIONS

Essential Elements:
- The student will apply music reading skills to the performance of a short accompanied song. (NS 5A, 5B, 5E)

Focus:
Read your own vocal part in an accompanied song.

Teaching Tips:
- Follow the suggested teaching sequence above.
- Remind singers to use tall, round vowels.
- Do not sing the text until singers are secure on pitches and rhythm.

Teaching Tips: (continued)

Higher Level Thinking:

Sight-reading an accompanied song requires analysis and synthesis of all previously learned skills and information. Previous knowledge is being applied to a new situation.

EE6: GOALS AND OVERVIEW

In this chapter, the choir will be introduced to the concept of whole steps and half steps, as they relate to the construction of a C major scale. This is a very important concept, since subsequent scales and keys are based upon these principles.

In addition, this chapter presents the concept of singing in parts through the use of bracketed systems. A careful sequence of instruction is presented for 2-part treble, 2-part tenor bass, and 4-part mixed choirs.

ESSENTIAL ELEMENTS AND NEW CONCEPTS

Voice:
The student will develop the posture and breath control needed to support choral tone.
(NS 1A)

* Practice the five basic vowels. Stress "ee" and "eh" vowels.

Theory:
The student will sing and recognize whole steps and half steps in a C Major scale. (NS 5C, 5D)
(Extension) The student will use music notation software to notate a C major scale. (NS 4C)

* Half step, whole step, major scale
* C major scale

Sight-Reading:
The student will apply knowledge of whole and half steps (NS 5A, 5B, 5E)

* Practice with half steps and whole steps in the key of C
* Combinable exercises in the key of C

Performance:
The student will become familiar with the musical terms *ensemble*, *slur*, *legato*, presented on this page. (NS 5C)
The student will become familiar with plainsong or chant. (NS 6B, 6C, 9A).
(Extension) The student will translate monophonic movement in music into an interpretive drawing or dance. (NS 8A)

* Sing unison melodies
* Combine melodies in 2- or 4-part bracketed systems.
* Add text to a 2- or 4-part exercise to create a short a cappella song.

POSTURE/BREATH/TONE

Posture: Check your posture and ask yourself these questions.
- Stand with feet apart (Is your weight balanced?)
- Knees unlocked (Can you bend them easily?)
- Back straight (Are you standing erect comfortably and not stiff?)
- Head erect (Is your chin level, and not too far up or down?)
- Rib cage lifted (Is your chest high and able to expand?)
- Shoulders relaxed (Are they comfortably down, not too far forward or back?)
- Hands at your side (Relaxed and free of tension)

Just like athletes, singers need to prepare themselves for the physical process of singing. Performance, whether on the playing field or in a concert, will suffer if the body is not sufficiently prepared or involved.

Practice good posture, good breathing, and good vocal habits every day in rehearsal, and these good habits will be there to help you succeed in performance.

1. Lift the left shoulder high and then let it fall. Repeat with the right shoulder and then both shoulders. Drop the head gently to the chest, and then let it roll to the right and then the left. Stretch overhead, then fall forward like a rag doll and then gradually stand up to a good singing posture.

Breath: Practice breathing exercises every day. Apply this practice to all your music making, sight-reading music, rehearsing music, performing music.

2. When people are suddenly startled, they usually take a deep natural breath very quickly. Take a "surprised" breath. Notice the action of the *diaphragm*.

3. Imagine that there is an elevator platform at the bottom of your lungs. Drop the platform toward the floor as you inhale. Inhale 4 counts, exhale 4 counts. Repeat with 5, then 6 counts.

Tone: Review the 5 basic vowels used in choral singing: ee, eh, ah, oh, oo. Most other vowel sounds are modifications or blends of these five sounds.

| ee | eh | ah | oh | oo |

TEACHING SUGGESTIONS

Essential Elements:
- The student will develop the posture and breath control needed to support choral tone. (NS 1A)

Focus:
Develop the skills needed to sing the "ee" and "eh" vowels with beautiful tone.

Teaching Tips:
Note: Much of the text on this page and throughout the Voicebuilder sections is designed to be practiced by the students as the teacher models and directs the students orally. Use the printed material for extra reinforcement and review as needed.

The "ee" and "eh" vowels should be sung with vertical mouth space, relaxed jaw and space inside the mouth.

TONE

4. Practice the following exercise and notice the difference between the vowels. With all the vowels remember to keep a relaxed jaw and vertical space inside the mouth.

   Especially on the "ee" and "eh" vowels, it is important to keep the corners of the mouth from spreading outward. If you sing the "ee" and "eh" vowel with a horizontal rather than a vertical mouth shape, it may sound flat and disrupt the tone quality you are trying to achieve.
   • For the "ee" vowel, keep the corners of your mouth tucked in.
   • For the "eh" vowel, the mouth is opened slightly more than the "ee".
   • For both, use space inside the mouth.
   • Repeat the exercise at different pitch levels, both higher and lower.

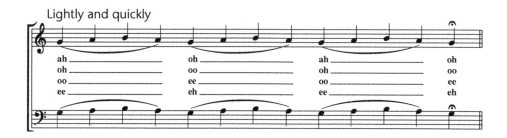

5. Practice the following descending scale.
   • Take an expanded rib cage breath and try to sing the entire pattern on one breath.
   • Keep a relaxed jaw and vertical space inside your mouth. Keep the corners of your mouth from spreading outward.
   • Change smoothly from one vowel to the next. Blend your voice with those around you.
   • Repeat at different pitch levels, both higher and lower.

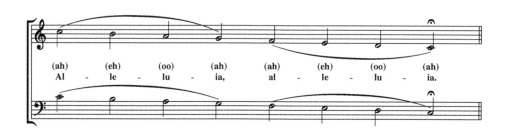

Teaching Tips: *(continued)*

Follow the procedures specified above.
• *Stress the importance of keeping the corners of the mouth from spreading outward on the "ee" and "eh" vowels.*
• *Remember to keep the "eh" in "alleluia" a pure vowel. Do not let it become "ay."*
• *Review the "ah" vowel. Keep the "ah" tall, especially on the final syllable of "alleluia." Avoid "yuh."*

Extension:
Find and mark other "ee" and "eh" vowels in the songs which follow in this chapter and all other music you are performing.

WHOLE STEPS • HALF STEPS

Remember that *key* is the importance of one pitch over the others in a scale. The keynote is described as the home tone. So far, we've learned the *key of C*, which if played on the piano would begin on C and progress stepwise using only the white keys of the piano.

⊔ = whole step

∨ = half step

These steps on the piano for the key of C are an arrangement of *whole steps* and *half steps*.

A *half step* is the smallest distance (or *interval*) between two notes on a keyboard.

A *whole step* is the combination of two half steps side by side.

A *major scale* is a specific arrangement of whole steps and half steps in the following order:

C Major Scale

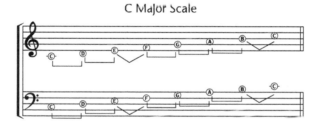

Check your knowledge!

1. What is a *half step*? What is a *whole step*?

2. What is a *major scale*?

3. What is the order of whole/half steps in a major scale?

TEACHING SUGGESTIONS

Essential Elements:
- The student will sing and recognize whole steps and half steps in a C Major scale. (NS 5C, 5D)
- (Extension) The student will use music notation software to notate a C major scale. (NS 4C)

Focus:
The major scale is a specific arrangement of whole steps and half steps.

Teaching Tips:
- Review key and keynote definitions as stated above.
- Define half step and whole step for the students. Demonstrate half and whole steps on the keyboard and use other visual reinforcement such as the graphic on this page, an overhead projector, or the chalkboard, etc.
- The answers to the Check Your Knowledge! section are located in the text above.

Extension:
- Guide students to correctly notate a C Major scale on manuscript paper, or in a music notation software program on the computer. After they have notated the scale, draw corresponding whole step and half step brackets.

WHOLE/HALF STEP PRACTICE

"Remind singers to
listen closely to each
other as they sing.
Half steps will be
challenging to tune
accurately."

TEACHING SUGGESTIONS

Essential Elements:
• The student will apply knowledge of whole and
half steps (NS 5A, 5B, 5E)

Focus:
Transfer knowledge of whole and half step notation
to a sung exercise.

Teaching Tips:
• The teacher may wish to substitute the pitch
names of the chosen pitch reading method to
the letter names used in this exercise. For example, the first line in movable "do" would read:
"do, re whole step, re mi, whole step, do re mi re
whole step, whole step, whole."
• This exercise may be sung on a daily basis as part
of a warm-up series.
• Return to this page often.

Student Book Page 35

MORE WHOLE/HALF STEP PRACTICE

When the tenor part is written in treble clef, there is sometimes a small "8" attached to the clef sign (see #4 and #5 below). This means that the notes are to be sung 1 octave (8 scale tones) lower. Even when the "8" is missing from the clef sign, tenors sing an octave lower. For example:

sounds

Sing each line separately and in any combination.

① ② ③ ④ ⑤ ⑥ ⑦ ⑧

"The combinability of exercises allows you enough variety to continue practicing a particular concept until it is internalized."

Teaching Tips: *(continued)*

- *Read and discuss the information about the notation of tenor lines that appears on this page.*
- *Perform each exercise separately using this sequence:*
1. *Chant rhythm of each line.*
2. *Chant pitch names in rhythm.*
3. *Sing pitches in rhythm using your chosen method.*
4. *Students sing one line while teacher sings a different line.*
5. *Divide class into two sections and sing two lines.*

Extension:
Ask students to identify the half steps before singing each exercise on this page. The teacher may create other exercises for students to practice labeling whole and half steps.

TREBLE • TENOR BASS • MIXED

The choral pieces on pages 37-40 were written for three different types of choral *ensembles*. An *ensemble* is a French term, and refers to a group of musicians performing together.
- Treble Chorus (soprano and alto)
- Tenor Bass Chorus (tenor and bass)
- Mixed Chorus (soprano, alto, tenor, bass)

Musical Terms:

slur - a curved line placed above or below a group of notes to indicate that they are to be sung on the same text syllable. Slurs are also used in instrumental music to indicate that the group of notes should be performed *legato* (or smooth and connected) or in the case of stringed instruments, with one stroke of the bow.

History: *Plainsong* or *Chant* was a style of singing which developed during the period of music history known as the Medieval era. A characteristic of Chant is the use of long groups of notes called *melismas* which were sung on one syllable, and often on the word "alleluia." These free-flowing melodies performed by solo voice (the *cantor*) and by the choir (the *schola*) were highly organized and structured, and important to the development of Western music. Chant continues to be a compositional device used by composers.

Chant exists in many non-Western cultures as well.

> "In many of the following chapters, performance material will be divided among three ensemble types. For extra practice in sight-reading, treble choruses can sing the SA and tenor bass choruses may sing the TB of mixed chorus songs. Likewise, sopranos and altos and tenors and basses of mixed choruses may sing the treble and tenor bass repertoire."

TEACHING SUGGESTIONS

Essential Elements:
- The student will become familiar with the musical terms ensemble, slur and legato presented above. (NS 5C)
- The student will become familiar with plainsong or chant. (NS 6B, 6C, 9A).
- (Extension) The student will translate monophonic movement in music into an interpretive drawing or dance. (NS 8A)

Focus:
Perform a short a cappella partsong.

Teaching Tips:
- *This page is a preparation page for the actual performance pages which follow.*
- *Discuss the three types of ensembles listed above.*
- *Discuss the concepts of slur and legato as specified in the text.*
- *Read information about chant on this page.*
- *Turn to the appropriate page for treble chorus student p. 37, tenor bass chorus p. 38, or mixed chorus student p. 39-40.*

Extension:
- *Play a recording of chant and ask students to describe what they hear. Can they identify the melismas? Non-western examples of chant and melisma include the music of Tibetan monks and the music of India.*
- *Play a recording of chant and ask students to translate what they hear into a drawing or dance.*

TREBLE CHORUS

First, sight-read the individual lines or *melodies*. Chant the rhythm first, then add pitch. Repeat as necessary. After you can sing each line separately, combine the lines. When two or more melodies are sung together, the result is *harmony*.

In the music below, lines #1 and #2 that you have just sung, are combined. Notice how the parts are bracketed together. Lines that are bracketed together are to be sung at the same time.

Now lines #1 and #2 are given text.

Soprano: Sing al-le-lu - ia, al-le-lu, al-le-lu, sing al-le-lu - ia, al-le-lu - ia!

Alto: Sing al-le-lu - ia, __ sing, sing, sing al-le-lu - ia, al - le-lu - ia!

"Encourage singers to use good posture, expanded ribcage breathing, accurate intonation of whole and half step interval, and tall uniform vowels."

Teaching Tips: (continued)

• Follow the suggested sequence on this page which is designed to introduce young singers to the performance of a short part song.

TENOR BASS CHORUS

First, sight-read the individual lines or *melodies*. Chant the rhythm first, then add pitch. Repeat as necessary. After you can sing each line separately, combine the lines. When two or more melodies are sung together, the result is *harmony*.

In the music below, lines #1 and #2 that you have just sung, are combined. Notice how the parts are bracketed together. Lines that are bracketed together are to be sung at the same time.

Now lines #1 and #2 are given text.

Tenor: Sing al - le - lu - ia, sing al - le - lu - ia, al - le - lu - ia, al - le - lu, al - le - lu - ia.

Bass: Sing al - le - lu - ia, sing al - le - lu - ia, sing al - le - lu, al - le - lu - ia.

> "Encourage singers to use good posture, expanded ribcage breathing, accurate intonation of whole and half step intervals, and tall uniform vowels."

Teaching Tips: (continued)

• *Follow the suggested sequence on this page which is designed to introduce young singers to the performance of a short part song.*

MIXED CHORUS

First, sight-read the individual lines or *melodies*. Chant the rhythm first, then add pitch. Repeat as necessary. After you can sing each line separately, combine the lines. When two or more melodies are sung together, the result is *harmony*.

In the music below, lines #1 through #4 that you have just sung, are combined. Notice how the parts are bracketed together. Lines that are bracketed together are to be sung at the same time.

NOTE: You may sing either SAT or SAB, if you lack sufficient voices for 4-part music.

"Encourage singers to use good posture, expanded ribcage breathing, accurate intonation of whole and half step intervals, and tall uniform vowels."

Teaching Tips: (continued)

• Follow the suggested sequence on this page which is designed to introduce young singers to the performance of a short part song.

Student Book Page 40

MIXED CHORUS

Now lines #1 through #4 are given text.

NOTE: Throughout this text, for extra practice in sight-reading, treble choruses can sing the SA and Tenor Bass Choruses can sing the TB of the Mixed Chorus songs. Sopranos and Altos in Mixed Choirs can sight-read Treble Chorus songs, and Tenors and Basses can sight-read the TB material.

EE7: GOALS AND OVERVIEW

This chapter presents review and practice of skills learned thus far in the course. In addition, the students are given three short a cappella songs in treble, tenor bass, and mixed voicings to allow them to apply their sight-reading skills to a performance situation.

The teacher may use this opportunity to assess student learning on a large group, small group, or individual basis.

ESSENTIAL ELEMENTS AND NEW CONCEPTS

Voice:

The student will develop the posture and breath control needed to support choral tone. (NS 1A)
The student will sing with tall, uniform vowels. (NS 1A)

- Practice concepts of good posture, expanded rib cage breathing, breath support, and tall, uniform vowels
- Expand repertoire of vocalises

Theory:

The student will describe and review elements of musical notation (NS 5C, 5D)

- Review concepts presented in Chapters 1-6

Sight-Reading:

The student will read and sing rhythmic and melodic patterns. (NS 1E)
The student will develop intonation awareness through the study of whole steps and half steps. (NS 1A)

- Practice sight-reading stepwise melodies in the key of C
- Practice reading rhythmic and melodic exercises which use quarter, half, and whole note patterns
- Practice half step and whole step patterns in the key of C
- Sight-read combinable exercises in the key of C

Performance:

The student will develop performance techniques of a variety of musical periods. (NS 1E)
The student will apply music reading skills to the performance of a short a cappella song. (NS 5A, 5B, 5E)
(Extension) The student will define and aurally discriminate between monophony, homophony, and polyphony. (NS 6A)
(Extension) The student will discuss poetic imagery in the poem "Winter" by Alfred Lord Tennyson. (NS 8B)

- Treble, Tenor Bass, and Mixed choirs apply skills by sight-reading and performing short a cappella songs

POSTURE/BREATH/TONE

Posture/ Breath:

1. Stretch overhead, side to side, up and down, then shake to relax any tight muscles.

2. Raise your arms overhead, stretching the fingers out in all directions. Bring the arms back to the side, relaxed and free of tension.

3. Exhale all your air. Wait for a moment until your body lets you know it needs air. Allow the air to flow in without effort. Repeat.

4. Imagine you have a milkshake as large as the room. Hold your arms in front of you around this giant "milkshake" and drink in the air through a giant "straw."

5. Place your fingertips just below your rib cage and take a "surprised" breath. Notice the movement of the diaphragm.

6. Inhale while raising your arms overhead (notice the expanded rib cage). Exhale on a hiss in this pattern, while slowly lowering your arms:

ss ss ss ss ss _____ (repeat 1 or 2 times on each breath)

Tone: As you practice the following exercises, remember
• Keep a relaxed jaw and vertical space inside the mouth.
• Don't let the corners of the mouth spread outward.
• Listen, tune and blend your voice with other voices around you.
• Take a full, expanded rib cage breath before each repetition.
• Repeat at different pitch levels, both higher and lower.

7. Inhale while raising arms overhead and sing on "hoo" as you lower your arms. Sing short, detached sounds.

Lightly and detached

hoo hoo hoo hoo   hoo   hoo hoo hoo hoo   hoo   hoo hoo hoo hoo   hoo

TEACHING SUGGESTIONS

Essential Elements:
• *The student will develop the posture and breath control needed to support choral tone.*
  (NS 1A)
• *The student will sing with tall, uniform vowels.*
  (NS 1A)

Focus:
Review and practice information learned in chapters 1-6.

Teaching Tips:
• *This chapter presents a repertoire of breathing exercises and vocalises which may be used for daily vocal warm-ups and other rehearsal occasions.*
• *Don't try to use all these exercises at once. Spread them out over the rehearsal or use in different rehearsals.*
• *Adapt exercises as needed for your particular situation.*

Student
Book Page
42

TONE

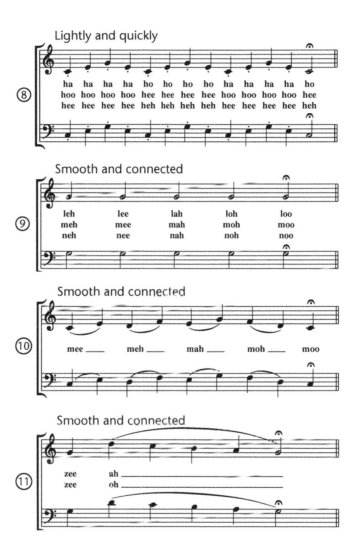

Lightly and quickly

⑧
ha ha ha ha ho ho ho ho ha ha ha ha ho
hoo hoo hoo hoo hee hee hee hee hoo hoo hoo hoo hee
hee hee hee hee heh heh heh heh hee hee hee hee heh

Smooth and connected

⑨
leh   lee   lah   loh   loo
meh   mee   mah   moh   moo
neh   nee   nah   noh   noo

Smooth and connected

⑩
mee ____ meh ____ mah ____ moh ____ moo

Smooth and connected

⑪
zee   ah _____
zee   oh _____

Teaching Tips: *(continued)*

- *The vowels should be sung with vertical mouth space, relaxed jaw and space inside the mouth.*
- *Stress the importance of keeping the corners of the mouth from spreading outward.*
- *The "h" in front of the vowels in exercise 8 discourages the use of a glottal stop.*
- *Exercises 9-11, in addition to helping the student create a smooth legato tone, help to develop resonance.*

Check your knowledge!

1. What is *rhythm*?

2. Define *beat*.

3. How many half notes equal the same duration as a whole note?

4. How many quarter notes equal the same duration as a half note?

5. How many quarter notes equal the same duration as a whole note?

6. How many lines and spaces does a *staff* have?

7. Give another name for *G clef*. Give another name for *F clef*. Define both clefs.

8. Name the pitch which may be written on its own little line in either clef.

9. What are the vertical lines that divide a staff into smaller sections?

10. Name the smaller divided sections of a staff.

11. How can you tell the end of a section of a piece of music?

12. Describe *meter*. What are the numbers that identify the meter?

13. Describe the following meters:

14. What is *pitch*?

15. Define *scale*. What is the Italian word for *scale* and its definition?

16. Describe *key*. Describe *keynote*.

17. What is *half step*? What is a *whole step*?

18. What is a major scale?

19. What is the order of whole/half steps in a major scale?

20. What is a *slur*?

21. What is an *octave*?

22. Define *soprano, alto, tenor, bass*.

TEACHING SUGGESTIONS

Essential Elements:
• The student will describe and review elements of musical notation. (NS 5C, 5D)

Focus:
Review information learned in chapters 1-6.

Teaching Tips:
Answers: (page number refers to student text.)
1. Rhythm is organization of sound lengths (duration). (p. 2)
2. Beat is a steadily recurring pulse. (p. 2)
3. 2
4. 2
5. 4
6. 5 lines and 4 spaces
7. G clef = treble clef; F clef = bass clef. A clef is a symbol that identifies a set of pitches. (p. 7)
8. Middle C (page 7).
9. Bar line (p 12)
10. Measure (p. 12)
11. Double bar (p. 12)
12. Meter is a form of rhythmic organization; a time signature (p. 12)

13. $\frac{4}{4}$ = four beats per measure, quarter note receives the beat; $\frac{3}{4}$ = three beats per measure, quarter note receives the beat; $\frac{2}{4}$ = two beats per measure, quarter note receives the beat. (p. 12)
14. Pitch is the highness or lowness of musical sound. (p. 24)
15. An inventory or collection of pitches. "Scala" means ladder. (p 24.)
16. The importance of one pitch over the others in a scale. The keynote is the home tone. (p. 24)
17. A half step is the smallest distance or interval between two notes on a keyboard. A whole step is a combination of two half steps side by side. (p. 33)

18. A specific arrangement of whole steps and half steps. (p. 33)
19. Whole whole half whole whole whole half. (p. 33)
20. A curved line placed above or below a group of notes to indicate that they are to be sung on the same syllable. Also to indicate legato. (p. 36)
21. An octave is the distance between eight scale tones. (p. 35)
22. Soprano is the highest treble voice, usually written in treble clef. Alto is a treble voice that is lower than the soprano, usually written in treble clef. Tenor is a male voice written in bass or treble clef. Bass is a male voice that is lower than a tenor, written in bass clef. (p. 26)

REVIEW AND PRACTICE

Practice naming these notes.

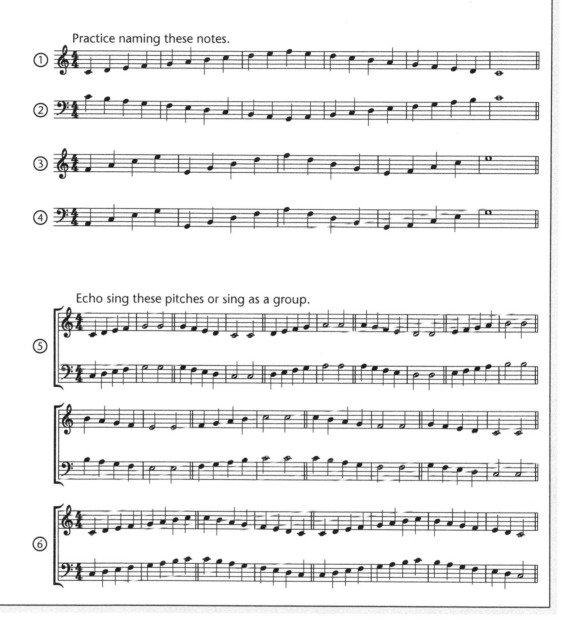

Echo sing these pitches or sing as a group.

TEACHING SUGGESTIONS

Essential Elements:

• The student will read and sing rhythmic and melodic patterns. (NS 1E)

• The student will develop intonation awareness through the study of whole steps and half steps. (NS 1A)

Focus:

Apply sight-reading information learned in chapters 1-6.

Teaching Tips:

• Practice naming the notes (exercise 1-4) and echo sing the patterns. (exercise 5-6)

• When echo singing, teachers should model beautiful singing tone and students should echo in the same tone.

• Some groups may be able to sight-read all three of the following pages.

REVIEW AND PRACTICE

Clap, tap, or chant (Can you describe these time signatures?)

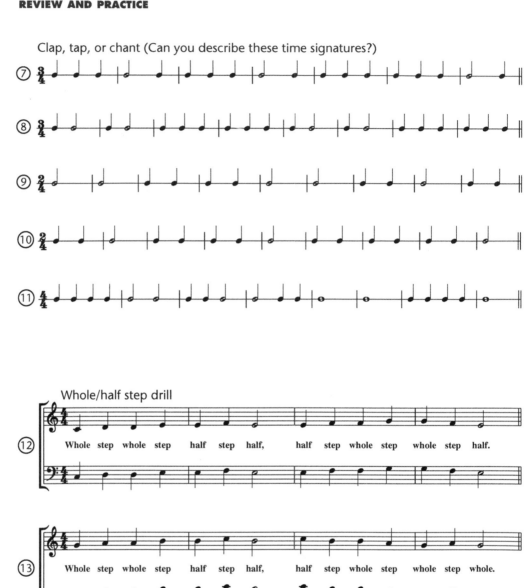

Whole/half step drill

"Half steps are the smallest interval we generally sing. Singers will often sing half steps too large."

Teaching Tips: *(continued)*

• *Encourage students to keep steady beat throughout these exercises and whenever sight-reading.*
• *Use your chosen method of rhythm reading.*
• *In exercises 12-13, stress accurate intonation.*

REVIEW AND PRACTICE

Sing each line separately and in any combination.

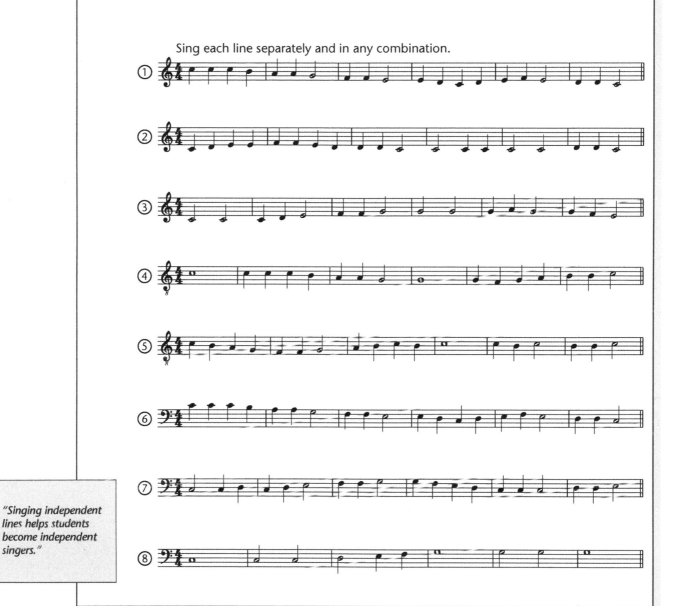

"Singing independent lines helps students become independent singers."

Teaching Tips: *(continued)*

- *These combinable exercises are further practice of melody and harmony. Note that any line may be combined with any other exercise on this page.*
- *Caution: Do not combine lines before the singers are ready. A suggested procedure follows:*
1. *Chant rhythm of each line.*
2. *Chant pitch names in rhythm.*
3. *Sing pitches in rhythm.*
4. *Students sing one line while teacher sings a different line*
5. *Divide class into two sections and sing two lines.*
6. *Divide the ensemble into more parts as ready.*

- *Encourage all voices to sing all lines. Changing voices may find more success with exercises 4 and 5.*

MUSICAL TERMS

Musical Terms:

monophony – Music which consists of a single melody. From the Greek words meaning "one sound," *chant* or *plainsong* is monophony.

polyphony – Music that combines two or more simultaneous voice parts usually with different rhythms. From the Greek words meaning "many sounds," polyphony is sometimes called *counterpoint.*

homophony – Music which consists of two or more voice parts with similar or identical rhythms. From the Greek words meaning "same sounds," homophony could be described as being in "hymn-style."

Music History

Prior to 800 A.D. music was monophonic. The early stages of polyphony began in 800 A.D. and developed over the next several centuries. In the 18th century polyphony reached a high level of sophistication in the works of **Johann Sebastian Bach**.

Much music in the 19th Century (sometimes called the *Romantic Period*) was *homophonic*. Examples of homophonic music may be found in some of the piano works, songs, and choral works of **Frederick Chopin**, **Franz Schubert**, and **Johannes Brahms**.

TREBLE • TENOR BASS • MIXED

In the following short choral pieces for **Treble** and **Tenor Bass** Chorus, both entitled "Sing Alleluia," the style of the music is *polyphonic*; that is, the melodies of each part have different rhythms. In fact, the melodies even "cross" with the soprano going below the alto, and the tenor briefly going below the bass.

The piece for **Mixed** Chorus "Winter," is written in *homophonic* style; that is, the four parts have basically the same rhythm.

The author of the text of "Winter" is Alfred, Lord Tennyson (1850-1892), an English poet of the Romantic Period who often wrote on topics relating to nature.

As you sight-read these pieces, remember to:
• Chant the rhythm of each part. Repeat as needed to become accurate.
• Add the pitch. Repeat as needed.
• Combine the parts. Repeat as needed until secure.
• Add the printed text. Sing the dynamics and other musical style markings.
• Apply your knowledge of voice and use good breath support and tone quality. Listen for good intonation and blend.

TEACHING SUGGESTIONS

Essential Elements:
• The student will develop performance techniques of a variety of musical periods. (NS 1E)
• The student will apply music reading skills to the performance of a short a cappella song. (NS 5A, 5B, 5E)
• (Extension) The student will define and aurally discriminate between monophony, homophony, and polyphony. (NS 6A)

Focus:
Students will sing an a cappella song in parts.

Teaching Tips:
• Use this material for reference in presenting the songs on pages 48-50.

Higher Level Thinking:
• Performance of actual pieces is analysis and synthesis of all previously learned material.
• Previous knowledge is being applied to a new situation.

TREBLE CHORUS

Remember to sing dynamics in your performance:

f – *forte*; loud

p – *piano*; soft

Sing Alleluia

For SA a cappella

Words and Music by
JOHN LEAVITT

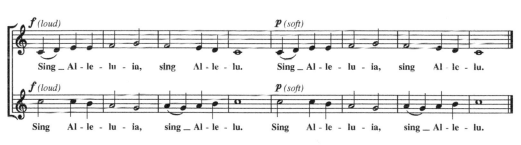

Teaching Tips: (continued)

- Chant the rhythm of the soprano part. Repeat as needed for accuracy.
- Add the pitch. Repeat as needed.
- Define unison singing as monophony. See student p. 47.
- Show a diagram on the board.

- Follow the same procedure when learning the alto part.
- When both parts are secure, combine them as written.

- Point out to the singers that when they combine both parts as written, they are now performing polyphony. See p. 47.
- Draw a diagram of polyphony.

- Add the printed text.
- Add the dynamics and other musical style markings.
- Use good breath support and tone quality. Listen for good intonation and blend.
- Return to p. 47 and review monophony, polyphony and introduce homophony.

Extension:

- Play recordings for the class of music written using the compositional techniques of monophony, polyphony and homophony. Suggested examples:
- Monophony - Gregorian Chant, unaccompanied folksongs.
- Polyphony - Bach: Little Fugue in G Minor, Kyrie from Bach B Minor Mass, any round or canon.
- Homophony - Brahms Liebeslieder Waltzes, any hymn.

TENOR BASS CHORUS

Remember to sing dynamics in your performance:

f – *forte*; loud

p – *piano*; soft

Sing Alleluia

For TB a cappella

Words and Music by
JOHN LEAVITT

Teaching Tips: *(continued)*

- *Chant the rhythm of the tenor part. Repeat as needed for accuracy.*
- *Add the pitch. Repeat as needed.*
- *Define unison singing as monophony. See student p. 47.*
- *Show a diagram on the board.*

- *Follow the same procedure when learning the bass part. (Tenors can sing one octave higher.)*
- *When both parts are secure, combine them as written.*

- *Point out to the singers that when they combine both parts as written, they are now performing polyphony. See p. 47.*
- *Draw a diagram of polyphony.*

- *Add the printed text.*
- *Add the dynamics and other musical style markings.*
- *Use good breath support and tone quality. Listen for good intonation and blend.*
- *Return to p. 47 and review monophony, polyphony and introduce homophony.*

Extension:

- *Play recordings for the class of music written using the compositional techniques of monophony, polyphony and homophony. Suggested examples:*
- *Monophony - Gregorian Chant, unaccompanied folksongs.*
- *Polyphony - Bach: Little Fugue in G Minor, Kyrie from Bach B Minor Mass, any round or canon.*
- *Homophony - Brahms Liebeslieder Waltzes, any hymn.*

Winter
For SATB a cappella

TENNYSON (Adapted)

Music by EMILY CROCKER

Full knee deep lies the win-ter snow, and the win-ter winds are sigh-ing.

Essential Elements:
• (Extension) The students will discuss poetic imagery in the poem "Winter" by Alfred Lord Tennyson. (NS 8B)

Teaching Tips: (continued)

• Sight-read using the following procedure:
• Chant each part separately in rhythm, repeating as needed.
• Add the pitch. Repeat as needed.
• Combine the parts. Repeat as needed until secure.
• Add the printed text. Sing the dynamics and other musical style markings.
• Use good breath support and tone quality. Listen for good intonation and blend.
• Groups with more experience may be able to sight-read all four parts simultaneously.

Extension:
• Draw students' attention to the poetic imagery in this poem (winter snow, tolling church bells, end of the year). How will their understanding of these images affect the way in which they perform this song?
• Ask students to research other poems by Alfred Lord Tennyson.

MIXED CHORUS

Teaching Tips: *(continued)*

- *If experience with polyphonic and monophonic music is desired, mixed choruses may sight-read the tenor/bass (p. 49), and treble songs. (p. 48)*
- *Compare the "Sing Alleluia" with "Winter." Note that the rhythm of the text in "Winter" is same in the different voice parts (homophony) but different in "Sing Alleluia" (polyphony). Monophonic experiences occur when a single voice part is sung alone.*
- *Use information on p. 47 of the student text to reinforce these concepts.*

Extension:

- *Play recordings for the class of music written using the compositional techniques of monophony, polyphony and homophony. Suggested examples:*
- *Monophony - Gregorian Chant, unaccompanied folksongs.*
- *Polyphony - Bach: Little Fugue in G Minor, Kyrie from Bach B Minor Mass, any round or canon.*
- *Homophony - Brahms Liebeslieder Waltzes, any hymn.*

EE8: GOALS AND OVERVIEW

In this chapter, the concept of major scale and key are transferred to the key of G. This requires introduction of the musical terms and symbols for *sharp* and *flat*, although the specific concept of key signature is delayed until Chapter 9.

ESSENTIAL ELEMENTS AND NEW CONCEPTS

Voice:

The student will articulate consonants precisely. (NS 1A)

The student will develop posture and breath control needed to support choral tone. (NS 1A)

- Holding music and maintaining good posture.
- Articulation
- New vocalises

Theory:

The student will sing and recognize whole and half steps in C major and G major scales. (NS 5C, 5D)

The student will correctly interpret the notation symbols of sharp, flat, and natural. (NS 5C, 5D)

- *Sharp, flat*
- G major scale
- Ledger lines

Sight-Reading:

The student will echo and read melodic patterns in the key of G. (NS 5B, 5C, 5D, 5E)

- Melodic patterns, and combinable exercises in G major.

Performance:

The students will become familiar with the musical terms which appear on this page and in the songs which follow. (NS 5C)

The student will apply music reading skills to the performance of a short a cappella song in the key of G. (NS 5A, 5B, 5E)

- mf, mp, legato, staccato, style marking, metronome marking
- A cappella songs for treble, tenor bass, and mixed choirs in the key of G, using stepwise melodic motion, and rhythm patterns limited to quarter, half, and whole notes

POSTURE/BREATH

1. Stretch your arms overhead, then bend at the waist and stretch toward the floor. Slowly rise up, one vertebra at a time until you are in a standing posture.

2. Rotate your shoulders, first your left, then your right, then both shoulders. Raise your head so that it is in line with the spinal column, and not tilted up or down. Remember to stand in a good singing posture:
   • Stand with feet apart (Is your weight balanced?)
   • Knees unlocked (Can you bend them easily?)
   • Back straight (Are you standing erect comfortably and not stiff?)
   • Head erect (Is your chin level, and not too far up or down?)
   • Rib cage lifted (Is your chest high and able to expand?)
   • Shoulders relaxed (Are they comfortably down, not too far forward or back?)
   • Hands at your side (Are they relaxed and free of tension?)

Holding Music: When you are singing your warm-up or performing a piece by memory, your hands should be at your sides. This position allows you to practice full, deep breathing without restriction.

When you are holding a folder or music in your hands, hold the music up, so that your head is erect and lined with the spine. This also allows you to watch the conductor. By keeping your elbows up and your arms away from your body, you allow your rib cage to be expanded, and full deep breathing to occur.

It's always best for each singer to have his/her own copy of music. Sometimes, however, this is not possible, and two or more singers have to share music. When this is the case, try to maintain a good singing posture. Hold the music up and out from the body, and if necessary turn slightly so that you are both facing the direction of the conductor.

ARTICULATION
We have concentrated on vowel sound so far (ee, eh, ah, oh, oo). The sung word in music requires articulation to produce the consonants. The articulators that we use in vocal music are the teeth, the lips and the tongue.

"Articulation requires muscle action."

3. For practice, repeat this short phrase quickly and precisely, concentrating on clean and clear articulation:

   The lips, the teeth, the tip of the tongue...the lips, the teeth, the tip of the tongue... (etc.)

TEACHING SUGGESTIONS

Essential Elements:
• The student will articulate consonants precisely. (NS 1A)
• The student will develop posture and breath control needed to support choral tone. (NS 1A)

Focus:
Good diction requires articulated consonants.

Teaching Tips:
• Remind singers about the importance of good posture.
• Demonstrate and practice good posture while standing, sitting and holding music.
• Read hints for holding music as presented in the student text.
• Introduce the concept of articulation as presented in the student text.
• Concentrate on the articulation in "the lips, the teeth, the tip of the tongue."

ARTICULATION

For each of the following exercises remember to:
• Take a full, expanded rib cage breath before each repetition.
• Sing pure vowels with a relaxed jaw and vertical space inside your mouth.
• Articulate all the consonants so they are clear and precise.
• Sing both consonants and vowels with the same breath support.
• Repeat at different pitch levels, both higher and lower.
• A fermata (⌢) over a note means to hold the note longer than its normal value.

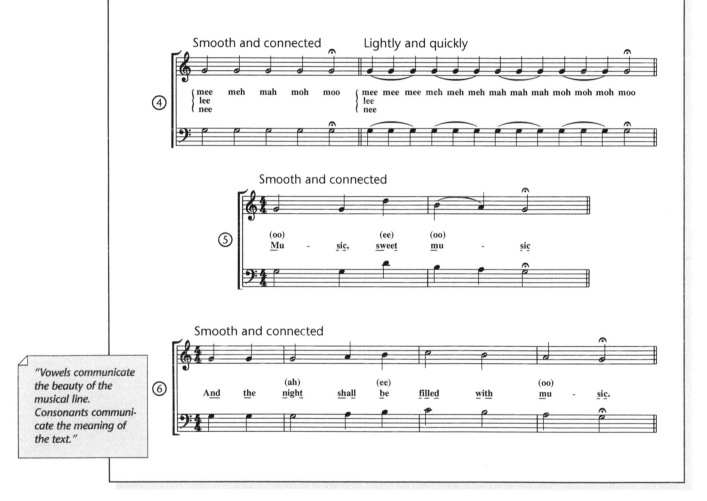

"Vowels communicate the beauty of the musical line. Consonants communicate the meaning of the text."

Teaching Tips: *(continued)*

• *This chapter presents a repertoire of vocalises which may be used at anytime for warm-ups.*
• *Don't try to use all these exercises at once. Spread them out over the rehearsal or use them in different rehearsals.*
• *Adapt exercises as needed for your particular situation.*

Extension:

• *Transfer the articulation of isolated consonants to actual words sung in music being rehearsed or performed.*

SHARPS & FLATS • REVIEW OF C MAJOR

You'll recall the order of whole/half steps for the C major scale:

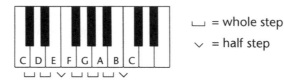

⌐⌐ = whole step

∨ = half step

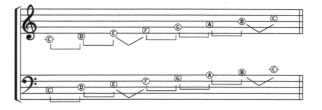

Music may be written with any note being the keynote. Because the order of whole/half steps must always be followed regardless of the keynote, the need arises for *sharps* (♯) and *flats* (♭).

A *sharp* raises the pitch one half step. This note, F♯ (F sharp), would be written with the sharp sign to the left of the notehead.

A *flat* lowers the pitch one half step. This note B♭ (B flat), would be written with the flat sign to the left of the notehead.

Practice
Name the following pitches:

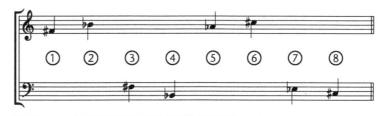

① ② ③ ④ ⑤ ⑥ ⑦ ⑧

TEACHING SUGGESTIONS

Essential Elements:
• The student will sing and recognize whole and half steps in C major and G major scales. (NS 5C, 5D)
• The student will correctly interpret the notation symbols of sharp, flat, and natural. (NS 5C, 5D)

Focus:
Major scales are made up of a specific order of whole steps and half steps.

Teaching Tips:
• *Review key and keynote.*
• *Review whole and half step information.*
• *Review the specific order of whole and half steps making up a major scale. Demonstrate at the chalkboard or keyboard.*
• *Introduce the concepts of sharps and flats.*
• *Practice naming the pitches in the Practice section of student page 54.*
• *Teach page 55 immediately after completing page 54. Both pages are designed to be presented as a unit.*

Student Book Page 55

THEORY BUILDERS 8

SHARPS & FLATS • KEY OF G MAJOR

To build a major scale starting on G, using the same arrangement of whole steps and half steps as in the key of C major, you'll notice the need for an F♯.

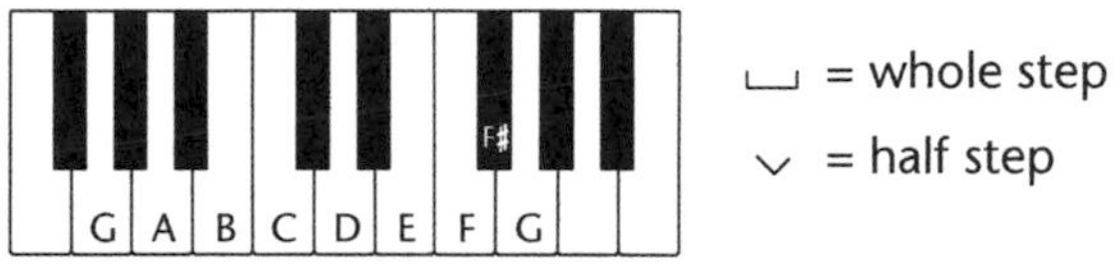

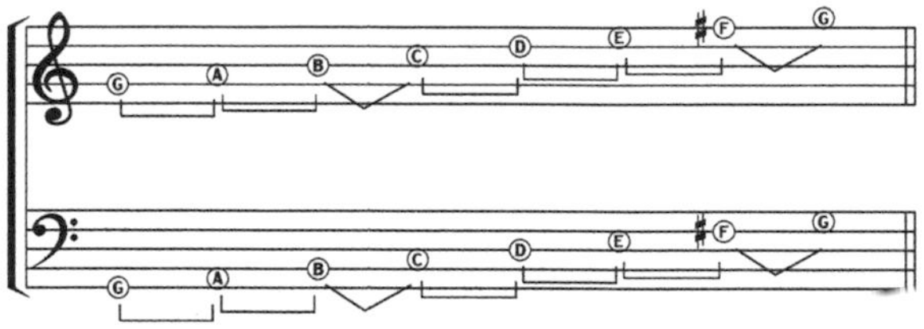

If we had written F - G, the *interval* (distance) between these two pitches would have been a whole step rather than the required half step.

Check your knowledge!

1. What is the order of whole/half steps for any major scale?
2. Does a *sharp* raise or lower a pitch? By how much?
3. Does a *flat* raise or lower a pitch? By how much?

Key of G Practice

Practice singing the key of G scale. Three octaves of the G scale are written below. Because of the wider range, you'll only be able to sing a portion of the three *octaves*, but take note of your own vocal range. What is your lowest note? Your highest note?

Remember that middle C can be written on its own little line in either clef. Other pitches may be written that way also. These little lines are called *ledger lines*. Ledger lines may be used to represent notes either above or below the staff.

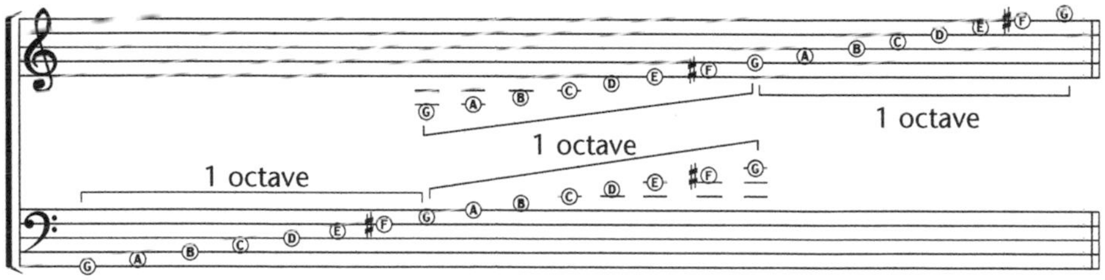

Teaching Tips: *(continued)*

- *Build a major scale starting on G using the same pattern of whole steps and half steps as in C major. Use the keyboard, chalkboard, and/or the graphic on this page as needed.*
- *Help the students to discover the necessity for an F sharp to create the major scale pattern.*
- *Use the keyboard to play a G scale with and without the F sharp so students can perceive the change in tonality.*

Answer the Check Your Knowledge! questions orally:
1. whole, whole, half, whole, whole, whole, half
2. A sharp raises a pitch by 1/2 step.
3. A flat lowers a pitch by 1/2 step.

- *Encourage students to identify their own vocal range within the three octave G major scale.*
- *Notice how notes other than middle C can be written with ledger lines.*

KEY OF G PRACTICE

Identify the following pitches in the key of G. Echo-sing or sing as a group.

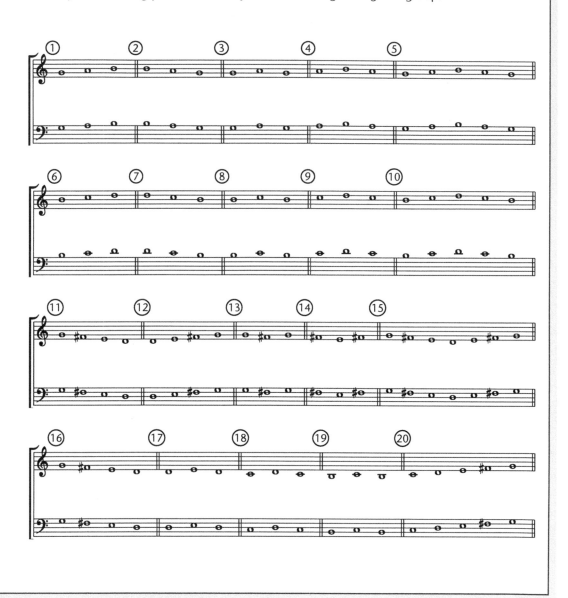

TEACHING SUGGESTIONS

Essential Elements:

• The student will echo and read melodic patterns in the key of G. (NS 5B, 5C, 5D, 5E)

Focus:

The student will practice connecting sound with symbol.

Teaching Tips:

• Echo-sing these patterns using your chosen pitch reading method.
• All students should sing exercises in an appropriate octave.
• Encourage changing voices to switch octaves as necessary.
• Note: Key signatures and the concept of accidentals lasting a whole measure will be presented in following chapters.

Student
Book Page
57

KEY OF G PRACTICE

Sing each line separately and in any combination.

①

②

③

④

⑤

⑥

⑦

⑧

"Singers may experience difficulty in transferring reading skills to a new key. Patience...this, too, will pass!"

Teaching Tips: *(continued)*

• *These exercises are further melody and harmony practice in the key of G. Note that any line may be combined with any other exercise on this page.*
• *Do not combine lines before the singers are ready. Here is a suggested sequence:*
   1. Chant rhythm of each line.
   2. Chant pitch names in rhythm.
   3. Sing pitches in rhythm.
   4. Students sing one line while teacher sings a different line.

   5. Divide class into two sections and sing two lines. Repeat with other combinations.
   6. Divide the ensemble into more parts as ready.
• *Encourage all voices to sing all lines. Changing voices may find more success with exercises 4 and 5.*
• *Always encourage students to sing expressively.*

MUSICAL TERMS

mf - *mezzo forte*, medium loud

mp - *mezzo piano*, medium soft

legato - smooth and connected. Sometimes indicated by placing the word *legato* above the staff or at the beginning of the song or section of a song. Also indicated by a *slur* above the notes to be performed legato.

From "Erin" for **Treble Chorus** on p. 59.

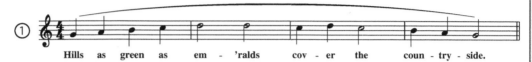

Hills as green as em - 'ralds cov - er the coun - try - side.

From "Sing Your Songs" for **Mixed Chorus** on p. 61.

Sing, sing your songs of sweet re - pose. _____

staccato - notes are to be performed short and detached. Usually written by placing a dot above or below the notehead:

From "Shipwrecked" for **Tenor Bass** Chorus on p. 60.

Good friends and all on you I call.

style marking - a word or phrase placed at the beginning of a song or section of a song to indicate in general, the way the piece should be performed. Sometimes style markings also include a *metronome marking* (♩ = 108) to indicate the tempo. This means 108 metronome beats per minute.

Identify the style markings for "Erin," "Sing Your Songs," and "Shipwrecked."

TEACHING SUGGESTIONS

Essential Elements:
- The students will become familiar with the musical terms which appear on this page and in the songs which follow. (NS 5C)
- The student will apply music reading skills to the performance of a short a cappella song in the key of G. (NS 5A, 5B, 5E)

Focus:
Perform a short song in parts using varied style markings.

Teaching Tips:
- Present the musical terms on the student page, and relate them to the performance material on pages 59-61 which follow.
- Sight-read the appropriate song (treble, tenor bass, mixed) on page 59-61. Then, return to page 58 and apply information from this page to the polishing of the selected song.

Student Book Page 59

TREBLE CHORUS

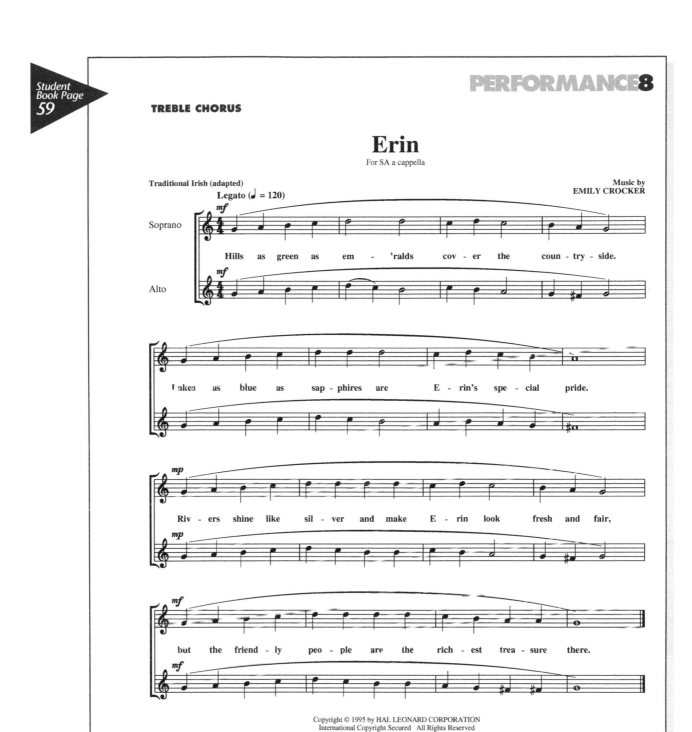

Erin

For SA a cappella

Traditional Irish (adapted)

Music by
EMILY CROCKER

Teaching Tips: *(continued)*

- *Sight-read the soprano line with all singers.*
  1. Chant the rhythm. Repeat as needed for accuracy.
  2. Add the pitch. Repeat as needed.
- *Follow the same procedure when learning the alto part.*
- *When both parts are secure, combine them as written.*
- *Add the printed text. Note that "Erin" is another word for "Ireland."*
- *Introduce new style markings (mf, mp, legato, metronome marking). Refer to student page 58.*

- *Teacher may model appropriate style markings. Students imitate.*
- *Use good breath support and tone quality by using correct breathing techniques and tall, uniform vowels. Listen for good intonation and blend.*

TENOR BASS CHORUS

Shipwrecked!

For TB a cappella

Traditional (adapted)

Music by
EMILY CROCKER

Boldly (♩ = 138)

Tenor: Good friends and all on you I call, lis-ten un-to

Bass: Good friends and all on you I call, lis-ten un-to

me. While I re-late my hard-ships and dan-gers of the

me. While I re-late my hard-ships and dan-gers of the

mp legato

sea. Ship-wrecked and lost was I, cast on the

mp legato

sea. Ship-wrecked in the bit-ter storm, I was cast on

mf   *cresc.*   *f*

shore, trav-eled to Can-a-da, there to ex-plore.

mf   *cresc.*   *f*

shore, took a trip to Can-a-da that coun-try to ex-plore.

Teaching Tips: *(continued)*

- *Sight-read the tenor line with all singers.*
  1. *Chant the rhythm. Repeat as needed for accuracy.*
  2. *Add the pitch. Repeat as needed.*
- *Follow the same procedure when learning the bass part.*
- *When both parts are secure, combine them as written.*
- *Introduce new style markings (mf, mp, legato, staccato, metronome marking). Refer to student page 58.*

- *Teacher may model appropriate style markings. Students imitate.*
- *Use good breath support and tone quality by using correct breathing techniques and tall, uniform vowels. Listen for good intonation and blend.*
- *Remember to use precise articulation.*

MIXED CHORUS

Sing Your Songs

For SATB a cappella

Words and Music by
JOHN LEAVITT

Teaching Tips: (continued)

• Sight-read using the following procedure:
1. Have each section chant the rhythm of their part and repeat as needed.
2. Add the pitch. Repeat as needed.
3. Combine the parts. Repeat as needed until secure.
4. Combine all parts. Repeat as needed until secure.
5. Add the printed text.
6. Groups with more experience may be able to sight-read all four parts simultaneously.

• Introduce new style markings (legato, mf, mp, metronome marking). Refer to student page 58.
• Use good breath support and tone quality by using correct breathing techniques and tall, uniform vowels. Listen for good intonation and blend.
• For extra practice and for a reinforcement of staccato and legato singing, sight-read the tenor bass song on student page 60 and the treble song on student page 59.

EE9: GOALS AND OVERVIEW

In this chapter the students are introduced to the concept of *key signature*, and the students continue to sight-read, practice, and perform music in the key of G major.

In addition, the choir is encouraged to continue applying the concepts of good tone quality, breathing, and articulation in warm-up exercises and performing.

The performance of a three-part canon offers the opportunity to experience polyphonic music.

ESSENTIAL ELEMENTS AND NEW CONCEPTS

Voice:
The student will articulate consonants precisely. (NS 1A)
The student will develop posture and breath control needed to support choral tone. (NS 1A)
The student will continue to build a repertoire of effective vocalises. (NS 1A)

- Practice good articulation, especially "s" and "st".
- Expand students' repertoire of vocalises.

Theory:
The student will correctly interpret the notation symbols of sharp, flat, and accidental. (NS 5C, 5D)
The student will understand and apply the concept of key signatures. (NS 5C, 5D)

- *Key signature*
- Half step, whole step melodic patterns in the key of G

Sight-Reading:
The student will read and sing rhythmic and melodic patterns in the key of G. (NS 5E)

- Combinable exercises in the key of G

Performance:
The students will become familiar with the musical terms which appear on this page and in the song which follows. (NS 5C)
The student will recognize and perform a musical example of canonic form. (NS 5D)
The student will apply music reading skills to the performance of a short a cappella song in the key of G. (NS 5A, 5B, 5E)

- Tempo, rit., a tempo, crescendo, descrescendo, diminuendo, repeat sign
- Canon, melody, harmony, texture, a cappella
- Three-part a cappella canon

VOICEBUILDERS9

Practice voice-builders everyday

POSTURE/BREATH/TONE

1. Lift the left shoulder high and then let it fall. Repeat with the right shoulder and then both shoulders. Drop the head to the chest gently and then let it roll to the right and then the left. Stretch overhead, fall forward like a rag doll and then gradually stand up to a good singing posture.

2. Imagine a balloon is attached to the top of your head. Allow it to lift your head until it is in alignment with your spine and your rib cage is lifted.

3. Sniff in air 2 times quickly, then puff out 2 times quickly.
   Sniff 3, puff 3
   Sniff 4, puff 4
   Sniff 4, puff 2
   Sniff 2, puff 4

   Notice how the air in your lungs feels buoyant. Try to maintain this buoyant feeling of breath support as you sing the following vocalises.

Tone/Articulation: In each of the following exercises remember to:
- Maintain a good singing posture.
- Take a full expanded rib cage breath before each repetition.
- Activate the *articulators* (lips, teeth, tongue).
- Produce good tone by concentrating on vowel formation and vertical space inside the mouth.
- Repeat at different pitch levels, both higher and lower.

TEACHING SUGGESTIONS

Essential Elements:
- *The student will articulate consonants precisely. (NS 1A)*
- *The student will develop posture and breath control needed to support choral tone. (NS 1A)*
- *The student will continue to build a repertoire of effective vocalises. (NS 1A)*

Focus:
Good diction requires articulated consonants.

Teaching Tips:
- *Remind singers about the importance of good posture.*
- *Demonstrate and practice good posture while standing, sitting, and holding music.*
- *Review the concept of articulation as presented in the student text.*

ARTICULATION

This exercise concentrates on "tip-of-the-tongue" consonants. Sing it quickly, lightly, and without a lot of jaw movement.

Lightly and quickly

⑤ la la la la la la la la la la la la la
na
ta
da

In the following exercise the "st" sounds of "first" and "star" should merge together to maintain a smooth legato phrase.

Legato

⑥ (ah) (ah) (ah) (ah) (ah) (ah) (ee) (oo) (ah)
Star light, star bright, first star I see ___ to - night.

Never prolong the "s" into a hiss. Move quickly on to the next vowel or consonant.

> "Vowels communicate the beauty of the musical line. Consonants communicate the meaning of the text."

Legato

⑦ (oh) (ah)
Soft ___ still - ness fills the night.

Teaching Tips: (continued)

- *This chapter presents additional vocalises to improve articulation.*
- *Adapt exercises as needed for your particular situation.*

Extension:

- *Transfer the articulation of isolated consonants to actual words sung in music being performed.*

ACCIDENTALS • KEY SIGNATURE

Let's review sharps and flats.

A *sharp* raises the pitch one half step. This note, F♯ (F sharp), would be written with the sharp sign to the left of the notehead.

A *flat* lowers the pitch one half step. This note B♭ (B flat), would be written with the flat sign to the left of the notehead.

There are two ways to write sharps and flats in music. One way is to write the sharp or flat to the left of the notehead as shown above. These are called *accidentals* because they are not normally found in the key in which you are performing.

The other way is to write a *key signature*. Since we know that the key of G will always use an F♯, rather than write the sharp sign on every F in the song, we simply write a sharp on F's line at the beginning of the song right after the clef sign(s) and before the time signature. (Note: The key signature is used with every clef sign in the song as a reminder.)

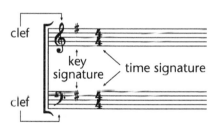

Placing an F♯ in the key signature indicates that the music is in the key of *G major* which always uses an F♯. Remember that the key of *C major* has no sharps or flats. Thus, the absence of sharps or flats in the key signature indicates that the music is in the key of C major.

Check your knowledge!

1. What is an *accidental*?

2. Where is a *sharp* or *flat* sign placed for a single note?

3. Where is a *key signature* placed?

4. What is the key signature for C major? For G major?

TEACHING SUGGESTIONS

Essential Elements:
• The student will correctly interpret the notation symbols of sharp, flat, and accidentals. (NS 5C, 5D)
• The student will understand and apply the concept of key signatures. (NS 5C, 5D)

Focus:
A key signature identifies the keynote of the music.

Teaching Tips:
• Review sharps and flats.
• Introduce the concept of accidentals. Note: This introduction to accidentals is limited to flats and sharps. The "natural" symbol is introduced later. Teachers should be encouraged to include a definition and examples of naturals if naturals appear in the music they are performing or if a teaching opportunity presents itself.

• Remind students than in the key of G, F is always sharp. A key signature is another way of indicating the constant F sharp. Teach the key signature information as presented in the student text.
• Review the information by discussing the Check Your Knowledge! questions. All answers may be found within the text on the above page.

KEY OF G PRACTICE

Sing notes and steps as indicated.

① G A whole step, A B whole step, G A B A whole step whole step whole.

② B C half step, B C half step, C B half step half.

③ C D whole step, D E whole step, C D E D whole step whole step whole.

④ G F♯ half step, F♯ E whole step, G F♯ E F♯ half step whole step half.

⑤ G F♯ half step F♯ E whole step E D whole step whole step whole step half.

Teaching Tips: (continued)

• *Practice these exercises using whole steps and half steps in the key of G. In this theory practice, the teacher may model, the students may sight-read, or the keyboard may be used to reinforce the learning.*

• *Remind students that the F sharp is in the key signature.*

• *Tenors may read treble or bass clef, switching octaves when it is out of their range (exercises 4-5).*

MORE KEY OF G PRACTICE

Sing each line separately and in any combination. Notice that not every melody starts on the keynote G. Identify the starting pitch of each melody and sing up or down the scale to locate the starting pitch.

TEACHING SUGGESTIONS

Essential Elements:
• The student will read and sing rhythmic and melodic patterns in the key of G. (NS 5E)

Focus:
Apply sight-reading information learned in chapter 8-9.

Teaching Tips:
• These exercises are further melodic and harmonic practice in the key of G. Note that any line may be combined with any other exercise on this page.
• Do not combine lines before the singers are ready. A suggested procedure follows:
  1. Chant rhythm of each line.
  2. Chant pitch names in rhythm.
  3. Sing pitches in rhythm.
  4. Students sing one line while teacher sings a different line.
  5. Divide class into two sections and sing two lines. Repeat with other combinations.
  6. Divide the ensemble into more parts as ready.

• Encourage all voices to sing all lines. Changing voices may find more success with exercises 3 and 4.
• Always encourage students to sing musically.
• Notice that not every melody starts on the keynote G. Establish the starting pitch of each line before singing.
• Challenge singers to find the line that quotes Beethoven's **"Ode to Joy."** (Theme from the Ninth Symphony). (Ex. 1 and 5)

TREBLE • TENOR BASS • MIXED

Musical Terms

tempo - speed of the beat

rit. - from the Italian *ritardando*, meaning gradually slower. When you see this term in music the *tempo* or speed of the beat gradually slows.

a tempo - from the Italian "to the time" meaning to return to the original tempo; often used after a *ritardando*.

——————————————— - a symbol meaning *crescendo*, or gradually louder.

——————————————— - the reverse of the above, *decrescendo*, or *diminuendo*, meaning gradually softer.

‖: :‖ repeat sign; repeat the section. If the first repeat sign is omitted, go back to the very beginning.

Music History

A *canon* is a musical form in which a melody in one part is followed a short time later by other parts performing the same melody. Sometimes the difference in time is as short as 1 beat, other times it may be several measures. Canons are sometimes called *rounds*, and you may know several already: "Row, Row, Row Your Boat," "Are You Sleeping," etc.

Canons are interesting musical forms because the *melody*, entering at staggered intervals produces *harmony*, when several voices are combined. This combination of voices in music is sometimes called texture. The earliest known canon dates to the 13th century and is called *Sumer is icumen in* ("Summer is a-coming in")

In the Middle Ages, a small place of worship was called a *cappella*, meaning "chapel". Later, the musicians (originally called the *schola*) who sang in these chapels became known as the *cappella*. After 1600 *a cappella* took on its present meaning, which is to sing unaccompanied by instruments.

JOYFULLY SING

Joyfully Sing, on p. 68 is a canon. As you learn this canon follow this procedure:
• Chant the rhythm of the unison melody, then add pitch. Repeat as needed to become secure. Add the text.
• Combine the three parts as a canon. After all three parts have sung the complete canon melody sing the ending.
• Sing musically with dynamics, good tone quality, and expression.

TEACHING SUGGESTIONS

Essential Elements:
• *The students will become familiar with the musical terms which appear on this page and in the song which follows. (NS 5C)*
• *The student will recognize and perform a musical example of canonic form. (NS 5D)*
• *The student will apply music reading skills to the performance of a short a cappella song in the key of G. (NS 5A, 5B, 5E)*

Focus:
Perform a short song in parts including a variety of style markings.

Teaching Tips:
• *Present and discuss the information on student page 67.*
• *Apply this information to the performance of the canon, "Joyfully Sing" on page 68.*

Joyfully Sing

For 3-Part a cappella

Words and Music by
EMILY CROCKER

Essential Elements:

- (Extension) The students will discuss the musical characteristics of a Renaissance polyphonic piece using appropriate musical terminology. (NS 6B)

Teaching Tips: (continued)

- Learn the unison canon using your chosen method of sightreading.
- Familiarize the students with the "road-map" of "Joyfully Sing" making sure they can interpret repeat signs accurately.

- Note that students move to a different line at each repeat as indicated in the score. Divide the ensemble into three equal groups. Group 1 enters on Part 1. When group 1 repeats, Group 2 enters on Part I, etc. When all groups have sung all three parts, perform the ending.
- Remind students that a canon is an example of polyphony. See p. 47 in the student text.
- Encourage students to sing musically with the dynamic and style markings as noted in the score.

- This piece was written for any combination of voices: mixed, treble or tenor/bass. The cue notes are to be used by changing voices.

Extension:

- Play a recording of or teach the singers to sing "Summer is a-coming in" (Summer is icumen in)- the earliest canon we know.
- Play a recording of an a cappella Renaissance polyphonic piece.

EE10: GOALS AND OVERVIEW

The chapters up to this point have used only quarter, half, and whole notes. By focusing so intensely on these rhythms, the students have had an opportunity to internalize and practice the steady beat and concentrate on developing pitch-reading skills without the distraction of complicated rhythm patterns.

In Chapter 10, the concepts of quarter, half, and whole rests are introduced and practiced.

In addition, students expand their knowledge of the vocal process by learning about the physical aspects of breathing.

ESSENTIAL ELEMENTS AND NEW CONCEPTS

Voice:
The student will develop an understanding of the breathing mechanism. (NS 1A)

- *Coordinated* breathing: inhalation, exhalation, release
- Action of the *diaphragm, intercostal muscles*

Theory:
The student will describe and demonstrate understanding of quarter, half, and whole rests. (NS 5C, 5D)
(Extension) The student will compose rhythm patterns using quarter, half, and whole notes and rests. (NS 4A)

- *Quarter, half, whole rests*

Sight-Reading:
The student will read and perform quarter, half, and whole note and rest rhythms accurately. (NS 5A)
(Extension) The student will compose rhythm patterns using quarter, half, and whole notes and rests. (NS 4A)

- Practice rhythm patterns using quarter, half, whole notes and rests.

Performance:
Students will combine text and rhythm. (NS 1E)

- 4-part speech chorus

POSTURE/BREATH

Posture: Check your posture and ask yourself these questions.
- Stand with feet apart (Is your weight balanced?)
- Knees unlocked (Can you bend them easily?)
- Back straight (Are you standing erect comfortably and not stiff?)
- Head erect (Is your chin level, and not too far up or down?)
- Rib cage lifted (Is your chest high and able to expand?)
- Shoulders relaxed (Are they comfortably down, not too far forward or back?)
- Hands at your side (Are they relaxed and free of tension?)

Coordinated Breathing
When you swing a bat or throw a ball, you use preparation, attack, and follow-through. It's the same with singing:

Inhalation - is your preparation. Just like the backswing of the racket, you must judge the distance, length and the loudness of the phrase you will sing.

Exhalation - Just like throwing a ball (attack), this is the part of breathing that requires the most coordination. When you throw a ball, your strength, knowledge, technical precision and discipline affect your accuracy. It's the same in breathing. The more you know, the more you've practiced, and the amount of effort you apply all combine to help you sing with a fully supported tone.

Release - As you end a musical phrase, follow through with the breath for a pleasing and accurate release. Just as you wouldn't choke your baseball swing, don't choke off the breath at the end of a phrase. When you release a phrase well, you also prepare for the next breath.

1. Breathe through an imaginary straw. Feel the expansion in your rib cage as your lungs fill with air. Sing the following pattern, and as you release the tone, also exhale the rest of your air. Repeat at different pitch levels.

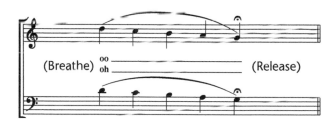

(Breathe) oo oh _____ (Release)

TEACHING SUGGESTIONS

Essential Elements:
- The student will develop an understanding of the breathing mechanism. (NS 1A)

Focus:
Diaphragmatic breathing is the foundation of good singing.

Teaching Tips:
- *Present student pages 69 and 70 in the same lesson.*
- *Teacher leads the students through the breathing exercises.*
- *Demonstrate the breathing exercises using the sports analogies mentioned on page 69, emphasizing preparation, attack and follow-through.*
- *This is a good time to stress that singing is a physical process and students must be physically involved as they sing.*

The Breathing Process

The physical aspect of breathing involves several different parts of the body.

During inhalation, the *diaphragm* muscle contracts, flattens and moves downward toward the feet. This motion pushes against the abdomen, pushing it outward. At the same time, the *intercostal muscles* (rib muscles) also contract, moving the ribs outward, expanding the rib cage. Since the lungs are attached to the diaphragm and the ribs, the lungs expand, and air rushes in.

When you sing, your exhalation is controlled, the abdominal muscles contract and the ribs stay expanded to provide resistance and control to the exhalation.

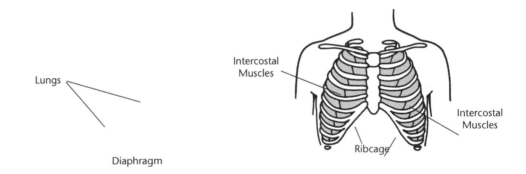

2. As you sing the following exercise, remember to:
   • Take a full expanded rib cage breath, remembering "prepare, attack, and follow-through" as you inhale, exhale on a tone, and release.
   • Breathe "on the vowel," i.e., if you are to sing an "ah," take your breath in an "ah" shape. This helps prepare you to sing with a relaxed jaw and vertical mouth space.

> "If you've tried everything else, remember, it just MIGHT be the breath! Good breathing can solve a multitude of problems!"

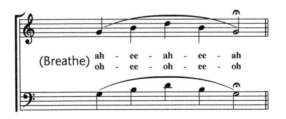

Teaching Tips: (continued)

• Stress that when singers use diaphragmatic breathing they can control exhalation more easily than if they use high chest breathing. The intercostal muscles are connected to the ribs and use of these muscles allows exhalation to be more controlled.
• Use a plastic model from the science class to demonstrate the muscular aspects of breathing.

RESTS

Rests are silences in music. They come in a variety of lengths, just like notes. These silences are just as important as the notes.

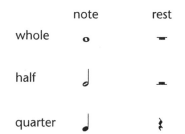

Rests and notes of the same name share the same duration.

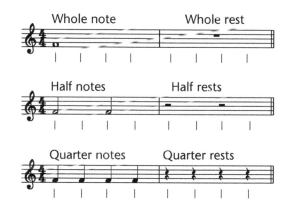

Check your knowledge!

1. Define *rests* in music.

2. Identify the following rests:

3. In $\frac{4}{4}$ meter, how many beats does a whole rest receive? A half rest? A quarter rest?

TEACHING SUGGESTIONS

Essential Elements:
• The student will describe and demonstrate understanding of whole, half and quarter rests. (NS 5C, 5D)

Focus:
Rests and notes of the same name share the same duration.

Teaching Tips:
• Read and discuss the material on this page.
• Review the material and answer the questions in Check Your Knowledge!
• The answers to the Check Your Knowledge! section are located in the text on this page.

PRACTICE WITH RESTS

Read each line (clap, tap, or chant)

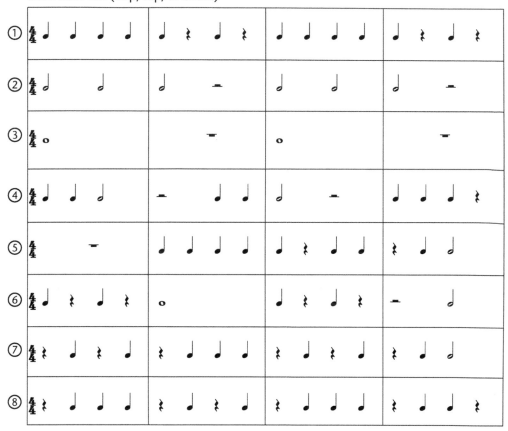

"Remember, silence is
as important as sound.
Perform rests accurately
and musically!"

TEACHING SUGGESTIONS

Essential Elements:
• The student will read and perform quarter, half, and whole note and rest rhythms accurately. (NS 5A)
• (Extension) The student will compose rhythm patterns using quarter, half, whole notes and rests. (NS 4A)

Focus:
The students will become independent readers.

Teaching Tips:
• Read the rhythm of each line while chanting in your chosen rhythm method and keeping a steady beat.
• Read several lines consecutively.
• Divide the singers into groups and perform two or more lines simultaneously.

Extension:
• Encourage the students to create and notate their own rhythm exercises using quarter, half, whole notes and rests.
• Perform the compositions in class.

Animal Song

For 4-Part Speech Chorus

Divide the choir into any number of groups up to four. Each group may chant one of the four numbered parts. Each part may proceed to the next part sequentially without break in rhythm. (example: group 1 sings parts 1-2-3-4, group 2 sings parts 2-3-4-1, etc.) Work for a sing-song kind of inflected speech at a light dynamic level. Practice slowly at first and gradually increase the speed of the beat.

Traditional Lyrics

Music by
JOHN LEAVITT

Quick inflected speech, lightly

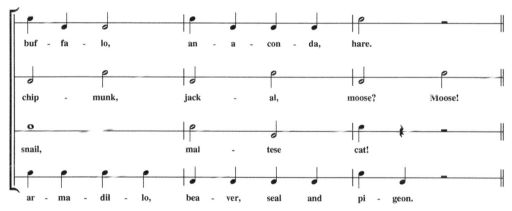

1 Al - li - ga - tor, hedge - hog, ant - eat - er, bear, rat - tle - snake,

2 Bull - frog, wood - chuck, wol - ver - ine, goose? Goose! Whip - poor - will,

3 Mud tur - tle, whale! Glow - worm, bat! Sal - a - man - der,

4 Ea - gle, king - er - on, sheep, duck and wid - geon, cou - gar,

buf - fa - lo, an - a - con - da, hare.

chip - munk, jack - al, moose? Moose!

snail, mal - tese cat!

ar - ma - dil - lo, bea - ver, seal and pi - geon.

TEACHING SUGGESTIONS

Essential Elements:
• Students will combine text and rhythm. (NS 1E)

Focus:
Vocal inflection can add humor and interest to a song.

Teaching Tips:
• Divide the choir into any number of groups up to four.
• Each group may chant one of the four numbered parts.
• Each part may proceed to the next part sequentially without break in rhythm, i.e. Group 1 sings parts 1-2-3-4, Group 2 sings parts 2-3-4-1, etc.
• Work for a sing-song kind of inflected speech at a light dynamic level.
• Practice slowly at first and gradually increase the speed of the beat.
• Stress articulation.

Extension:
• Encourage students to experiment with dynamic changes in this piece.

EE11: GOALS AND OVERVIEW

This chapter reviews information from chapters 1-10 (voice) and 8-10 (theory). It is also an opportunity for teachers to assess student learning and practice particular skills and concepts. If students have not mastered the material reviewed in this chapter, take the time to re-teach and practice rhythmic and melodic skills, as well as review specific knowledge-based material.

Voice:
The student will describe and demonstrate posture, breathing, vowel placement and articulation necessary for good tone. (NS 1A)

• Review chapters 1-10.

Theory:
The student will review basic notation. (NS 5C, 5D)

• Review chapters 8-10.

Sight-Reading:
The student will read and sing rhythmic and melodic patterns in the key of G. (NS 5E)

• Practice melodic exercises in key of G, using quarter, half, whole notes and rests.

Performance:
The student will apply music reading skills to the performance of a short accompanied song in the key of G. (NS 5A, 5B, 5E)
(Extension) The student will read and discuss the poetry of Robert Louis Stevenson. (NS 8B)
(Extension) Students will create musical compositions using Robert Louis Stevenson texts using computer-generated sound or other musical sources. (NS 4C)

• Students apply music reading skills to the performance of a short accompanied song in the key of G, using quarter, half, whole notes and rests.

REVIEW AND PRACTICE

Answer the following questions orally in large or small group discussion. Refer to previous chapters as needed.

1. Describe the steps for a good singing posture.

2. Why is good posture important in singing?

3. Describe a good singing posture for singing from memory. Describe a good singing posture for holding music. For sharing music with another singer.

4. What are the *five basic vowels* used in singing?

5. Why do we need *articulation* in singing?

6. What are the *articulators*?

7. What are the three stages of breathing for singing?

8. Describe the action of the *diaphragm* during breathing. The abdomen. The ribs. The lungs.

Tone/Articulation

Review all the elements of good singing in the following exercise:
- Take a full expanded rib cage breath, maintain the support while singing the phrase, and release.
- Breathe with your mouth in the shape of the vowel you are preparing to sing.
- Repeat at different pitch levels, both higher and lower.

Text by William Blake

(ah) (ah) (ah) (oh) (ah) (ah) (ah)
Ti - ger, ti - ger, burn - ing bright in the for - est of the night.

> "The concepts presented in this review chapter will continually appear in this text, with added information and refined terminology. Teachers are encouraged to constantly reinforce the elements of good singing in vocal warm-ups, rehearsals and performance."

TEACHING SUGGESTIONS

Essential Elements:
- The student will describe and demonstrate posture, breathing, vowel placement and articulation necessary for good tone. (NS 1A)

Focus:
Review information found in Chapters 1-10.

Teaching Tips:
- Answer the questions on this page orally in large group or cooperative learning situations.

Answers: (page numbers refer to the student text)
1. Stand with feet apart, knees unlocked, back straight, head erect, rib cage lifted, shoulders relaxed, hands at side. (p. 1)
2. Good posture helps produce good breathing. (p. 1)
3. Singing from memory - see #1. Singing while holding music: hold music up and out from the body so head is erect and aligned with the spine, elbows are up, arms away from the body, turn to face the conductor. Singing while sharing music: hold music up and away from body; turn so both singers are facing the conductor. (p. 52)
4. ee, eh, ah, oh, oo (p. 5)

5. Articulation produces the consonants in singing. (p. 52)
6. Articulators are lips, teeth, tongue. (p. 52)
7. The three stages of breathing for singing are inhalation, exhalation, and release. (p. 69)
8. Diaphragm muscle contracts, flattens and moves downward. The abdomen moves outward. The ribs move outward. The lungs expand. (p. 69-70).

- Apply all the elements of good singing to the exercise on student page 74.

REVIEW AND PRACTICE

Check your knowledge!

1. Name the order of whole steps and half steps for any major scale.

2. Define *sharp.* Define *flat.*

3. Name two ways sharps and flats can be placed in music.

4. Where is a sharp or flat sign placed in relation to the notehead.

5. Where is a *key signature* placed?

6. Name the key signature for C major. For G major.

7. What is the term for silences in music?

8. Identify the following rests:

9. How many quarter rests equal a half rest? How many half rests equal a whole note?

10. In $\frac{4}{4}$ meter, how many beats are in two whole notes?

Matching Drill

①    a) whole step

②   b) quarter rests

③   c) G major

④    d) half step

⑤    e) C major

⑥    f) F sharp

⑦   g) B flat

⑧    h) half rests

TEACHING SUGGESTIONS

Essential Elements:
• The student will review basic notation. (NS 5C, 5D)

Focus:
Review theory information presented in Chapters 8-10.

Teaching Tips:
Answer the Check Your Knowledge! questions in large group or cooperative learning situations.

Answers: *(Page numbers refer to the student text.)*
1. Whole, whole, half, whole, whole, whole, half (p. 54)
2. A sharp raises a pitch 1/2 step. A flat lowers a pitch 1/2 step. (p. 54)
3. Sharps and flats can be placed in the music as accidentals or in the key signature. (p. 64)
4. An accidental is placed to the left of the note-head. (p. 64)
5. A key signature is placed at the beginning of the song after the clef and before the time signature. (p. 64)
6. C = no sharps or flats; G = 1 sharp (p. 64)

7. Silences in music are rests. (p. 71)
8. Quarter, half, whole (p. 71)
9. Two quarter rests = a half rest. Two half rests = a whole note (p. 71)
10. There are eight beats in two whole notes.

Matching:
1=F, 2=E, 3=B, 4=D, 5=A, 6=G, 7=H, 8=C

Student
Book Page
76

KEY OF G • RESTS

Sing each line separately and in any combination.

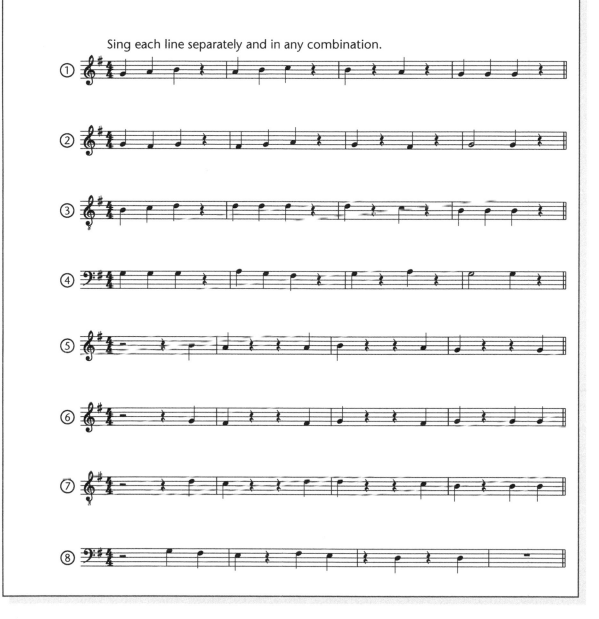

TEACHING SUGGESTIONS

Essential Elements:
• The student will read and sing rhythmic and melodic patterns in the key of G. (NS 5E)

Focus:
Apply sight-reading skills to reading music which includes rests.

Teaching Tips:
• These exercises are further rhythmic and melodic practice in the key of G. Note that any line may be combined with any other exercise on this page.

Suggested Sight-Reading Sequence:
1. Chant rhythm of each line.
2. Chant pitch names in rhythm.
3. Sing pitches in rhythm.
4. Combine lines as ready.

• Encourage all voices to sing all lines.
• Establish the starting pitch of each line before singing.
• It is especially important to establish and maintain a steady beat while performing these exercises.

UNISON VOICES

Music History: The text for this short piece was written by the Scottish poet Robert Louis Stevenson and included in his collection of poems for children: *A Child's Garden of Verses.* Stevenson, who lived from 1850-1894, also wrote two of the most famous novels ever written, *Treasure Island* and *The Strange Case of Dr. Jekyll and Mr. Hyde.*

Rain
For Unison voices and Piano

ROBERT LOUIS STEVENSON

Music by
EMILY CROCKER

The rain is fall-ing all a-round,

TEACHING SUGGESTIONS

Essential Elements:
• The student will apply music reading skills to the performance of a short accompanied song in the key of G. (NS 5A, 5B, 5E)

Focus:
Perform a short accompanied song which includes rests and varied style markings.

Teaching Tips:
• An important feature of this course is the inclusion of songs which illustrate concepts which are being studied in a musical context. Students can be successful and musically expressive even with songs of limited rhythm and range.

Suggested Sight-Reading Sequence:
1. Chant the rhythm of the melody.
2. Chant pitch names in rhythm.
3. Sing pitches in rhythm.
4. Add the text.
5. Add accompaniment and perform musically using the stylistic markings indicated in the piece.

• The cue size notes are for changing voices.
• Hold all notes for full value. Students will tend to shorten whole notes.
• Sing with tall round vowels.
• Pay special attention to the rhythm in phrases which begin on beat 2.

Essential Elements:
- (Extension) The student will read and discuss the poetry of Robert Louis Stevenson. (NS 8B)
- (Extension) Students will create musical compositions using Robert Louis Stevenson texts using computer-generated sound or other musical sources. (NS 4C)

Extension:
- Read and discuss the information about the poet Robert Louis Stevenson on student page 77.
- Encourage students to find other Stevenson poems and share them with the class. Some students may have read one of Robert Louis Stevenson's novels.
- Encourage students to create other musical compositions with computer-generated or other sound sources, using Stevenson's poetry as texts.

EE 12: GOALS AND OVERVIEW

The main goal of this chapter is the introduction of the concept of *interval*. The text material allows you to teach the concept of melodic intervals (2nd, 3rd, 4th, and 5th), which prepares the way for teaching *harmonic intervals* and *chords* in subsequent chapters.

Information about the *larynx* and the process of *vocalization* is also presented in this chapter. In addition to increasing the students' knowledge about the singing process, it is also a good opportunity for stressing vocal health.

ESSENTIAL ELEMENTS AND NEW CONCEPTS

Voice:
The student will continue developing breathing techniques emphasizing the open throat. (NS 1A)

The student will develop an understanding of the vocal mechanism. (NS 1A)

The student will develop an appreciation of the care needed for responsible use of the voice. (NS 1A)

(Extension) The student will relate information about the ears, nose, and throat to issues of voice production and vocal health. (NS 8B)

- *Vocalization, larynx, vocal folds*

Theory:
The student will sing and recognize melodic intervals. (NS 5E)

- *Interval, melodic interval*
- Practice identifying intervals of a 2nd, 3rd, 4th, and 5th.

Sight-Reading:
The student will sing and recognize melodic intervals. (NS 5E)

- Practice identifying and singing intervals of a 2nd, 3rd, 4th, and 5th in the keys of C and G

Performance:
The student will practice singing melodic intervals in a short a cappella song. (NS 5E)

- SA, TB, and SATB songs which prepare and practice interval skips in the key of G

POSTURE/BREATH

1. Stretch high overhead. Bend at the waist and gradually stand upright, one vertebra at a time. Nod your head "yes" several times, then "no."

2. Yawn-sigh

3. Imagine there is a milkshake as large as the room. "Drink" the air through a large straw. Exhale on a yawn-sigh.

4. Sip in air as though you were sipping water. Notice the cool feeling in your throat.

5. Breathe in with your lips in an "oo" shape, then sing the following exercise. Repeat the pattern at different pitch levels, both higher and lower. Open the vowel to an "ah" as you go higher and an "oh" as you go lower.

(Breathe on "oo") "oo"   (breathe)   *etc.*

6. Take a full, relaxed breath and sing on a staccato "hoo."

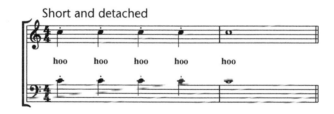

Short and detached

hoo   hoo   hoo   hoo   hoo

These exercises, and many others you will learn, contribute toward a relaxed and *open throat*. An open throat will help you produce a free, open tone that is not constricted or tension-filled, and will help keep your voice healthy. This is important as you develop resonance and flexibility in your voice.

TEACHING SUGGESTIONS

Essential Elements:
• *The student will continue developing breathing techniques emphasizing the open throat. (NS 1A)*
• *The student will develop an understanding of the vocal mechanism. (NS 1A)*
• *The student will develop an appreciation of the care needed for responsible use of the voice. (NS 1A)*

Focus:
An open throat will help produce a free, open tone.

Teaching Tips:
• *Teach student pages 79-80 in the same lesson.*
• *After establishing good posture and relaxation in exercises 1 and 2, perform exercises 3-6 to help the student experience an open throat.*
• *Students should experience the sensation of a relaxed open throat when performing these exercises.*

Vocalization

The source of vocal tone is the *larynx* (pronounced "LEH-rinks" and popularly called the "voice box"). The larynx is a part of the *respiratory system* and is not muscle, but is made of *cartilage*. The larynx is located midway between the mouth, nose and throat above, and the lungs and *trachea* (air passages) below.

You can find your own larynx by locating your "Adam's Apple." If your Adam's apple is not prominent, you can feel it if you lightly run your fingertip down the front of your neck from your chin, until you feel a hard structure with a sharp upper edge. If you hold your finger here while you say "ah" you can feel the vibration that the larynx produces.

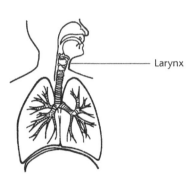

— Larynx

The Vocal Folds

The *vocal folds* (also called *vocal cords*) are a pair of muscles attached to the front and back of the larynx. They open and close somewhat like a valve – open for breathing, closed for singing (and speaking). Exhaled air passes between the gently closed vocal folds, causing them to vibrate. The number of vibrations per second produces pitch. The following illustration shows the vocal folds from above.

The Vocal Folds (seen from above)

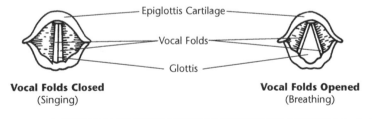

Epiglottis Cartilage
Vocal Folds
Glottis

Vocal Folds Closed
(Singing)

Vocal Folds Opened
(Breathing)

Essential Elements:
- (Extension) The student will relate information about the ears, nose, and throat to issues of voice production and vocal health. (NS 8B)

Teaching Tips: (continued)

- Now that the students have had some experience with singing they should be prepared to learn where the tone actually originates.
- Introduce this information by describing how sound is produced on various instruments, including violin, guitar, clarinet, trumpet, piano, etc.

- Relate vibrating vocal cords to a vibrating string.
- Read and discuss the information on student page 80, referring to the illustrations as needed. Models or charts from the science class may be available. Commercial videos showing the workings of the vocal mechanism may also be helpful in some situations. (See Bibliography on p. 203.)

Extension:
- Invite an ear, nose and throat specialist or a speech therapist to speak to the class about vocal health.

MELODIC INTERVALS

An *interval* is the measurement of distance between two pitches. When intervals are played in succession, they are called *melodic intervals*. Following are examples of intervals of 2nds, 3rds, 4ths, and 5ths.

Read the pitches, echo sing, or sing each example as a group:

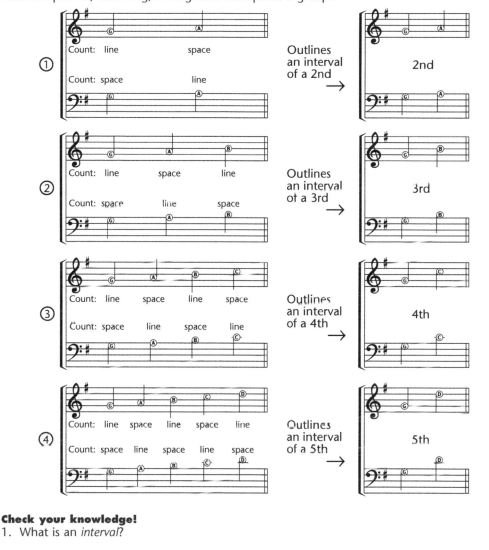

Check your knowledge!

1. What is an *interval*?

2. What are intervals played in succession called?

TEACHING SUGGESTIONS

Essential Elements:
• The student will sing and recognize melodic intervals. (NS 5E)

Focus:
An interval is the measurement of distance between two pitches.

Teaching Tips:
• *Define interval.*
• *Define melodic interval.*
• *Illustrate melodic intervals using the examples on this page.*
• *All the answers for Check Your Knowledge! are located within the text on this page.*

Extension:
• *Make a game of identifying intervals. Have one student write two notes on a staff on the chalkboard and a second student identify the interval.*
• *Extend practice to intervals greater than a fifth.*
• *Challenge students to measure intervals which descend as well as ascend.*

MELODIC INTERVAL PRACTICE

Identify the following intervals.

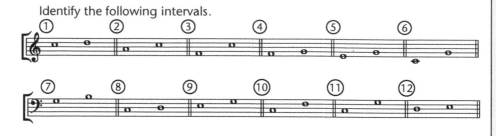

Sing the following interval drills.

13 C D, that's a sec-ond, C E, that's a third, C F, that's a fourth, C G, that's a fifth,

G C, that's a fifth, F C, that's a fourth, E C, that's a third, D C, that's a sec-ond.

14 G A, that's a sec-ond, G B, that's a third, G C, that's a fourth, G D, that's a fifth,

D G, that's a fifth, C G, that's a fourth, B G, that's a third, A G, that's a sec-ond.

TEACHING SUGGESTIONS

Essential Elements:
- The student will sing and recognize melodic intervals. (NS 5E)

Focus:
Apply melodic interval concepts to sight-reading practice.

Teaching Tips:
- Review knowledge of intervals by identifying melodic intervals in Exercises 1-12 in the student text on page 82.
- Practice 13 and 14 by rote, striving to internalize the sound of each interval.

KEY OF C INTERVAL PRACTICE

Practice the following exercises. Echo sing, or sing as a group.

Teaching Tips: (continued)

- Continue practicing melodic intervals.
- These exercises may be incorporated into your
  daily warm-up routine.
- Fluency in interval recognition and performance
  requires much repetition and practice.
- These exercises may be transposed to any key to
  accommodate range limitations.

Student Book Page **84**

KEY OF G INTERVAL PRACTICE

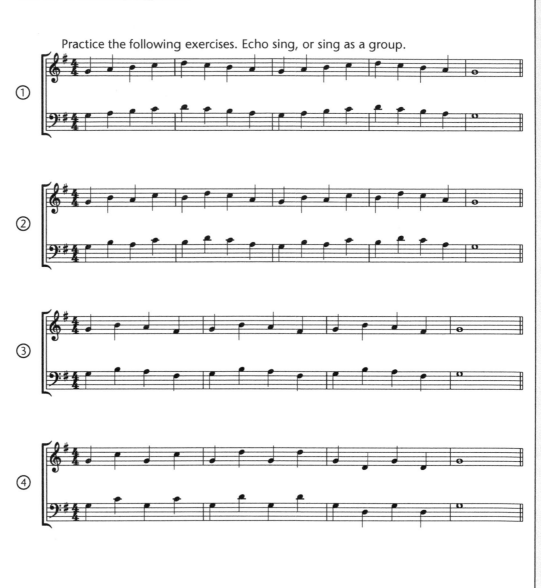

Practice the following exercises. Echo sing, or sing as a group.

Teaching Tips: (continued)

- This page presents the same material as on page 83, but in the key of G.
- These exercises provide additional melodic interval practice.
- Adapt these drills into other keys as needed to accommodate changing voices.

TREBLE CHORUS

Sing Hosanna

For SA a cappella

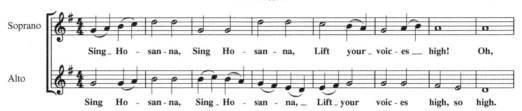

Soprano

Sing Ho - san - na, Sing Ho - san - na, Lift your voic - es high! Oh,

Alto

Sing Ho - san - na, Sing Ho - san - na, Lift your voic - es high, so high.

sing Ho - san - na, Sing Ho - san - na, Mu - sic fills the sky, the sky.

Sing Ho - san - na, Sing Ho - san - na, Music fills the sky, the sky.

TENOR BASS CHORUS

Sing Hosanna

For TB a cappella

Tenor

Sing Ho - san - na, Sing Ho - san - na, Lift your voic - es high! Oh,

Bass

Sing Ho - san - na, Sing Ho - san - na, Lift your voic - es high, so high.

sing Ho - san - na, Sing Ho - san - na, Mu - sic fills the sky, the sky.

Sing Ho - san - na, Sing Ho - san - na, Mu - sic fills the sky, the sky.

TEACHING SUGGESTIONS

Essential Elements:
• The student will practice singing melodic intervals in a short a cappella song. (NS 5E)

Focus:
Apply melodic interval practice to a performance situation.

Teaching Tips:
• Follow your established sight-reading procedure. For a suggested sequence, see student page 57.
• Sing with tall, uniform vowels on the word "Hosanna."
• The interval of a fifth is emphasized in this song. Work to sing it in tune with good breath support.
• The third and seventh scale degrees and all descending intervals tend to flat. Tune them carefully.

MIXED CHORUS

Sing Hosanna

For SATB a cappella

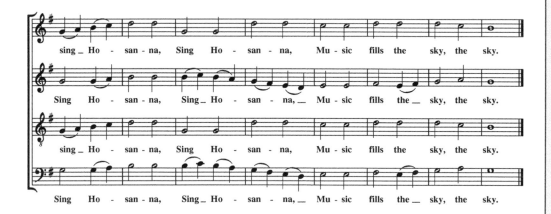

Teaching Tips: *(continued)*

- *Follow your established sight-reading procedure. For a suggested sequence, see student page 57.*
- *Sing with tall, uniform vowels on the word "Hosanna".*
- *The interval of a fifth is emphasized in this song. Work to sing it in tune with good breath support.*
- *The third and seventh scale degrees and all descending intervals tend to flat. Tune them carefully.*

EE 13: GOALS AND OVERVIEW

This chapter is a continuation of Chapter 12, and serves to prepare students to sing melodic interval skips and chords. Students have had a great deal of practice singing diatonic, stepwise melodies. Learning to sing melodic intervals of a 3rd, 4th, 5th, and larger is a very important step in learning to sight-read. Carefully assess their progress over the next few chapters. Sing the exercises and drills until this new concept is internalized.

Voice:

The student will sing with tall uniform vowels. (NS 1A)

The student will display the posture and breath control needed to support choral tone. (NS 1A)

- Review the five basic vowels: ee, eh, ah, oh, oo.
- Extend the principle of singing tall, uniform vowels to vowels other than the five basic vowels.

Theory:

The student will recognize harmonic intervals. (NS 5E)

- *Harmonic intervals*
- *Chords*

Sight-Reading:

The student will recognize and perform harmonic intervals in an ensemble. (NS 5E)

- Harmonic interval practice
- Chord building
- Combinable exercises which produce harmonic intervals and chords

Performance:

The student will become familiar with the musical terms which appear on this page and in the song. (NS 5C)

The student will apply music reading skills to an accompanied song in the key of G. (NS 5A, 5C)

The student will recognize form through repetition and contrast of musical material. (NS 5D)

(Extension) The student will discuss and analyze the characteristics of a madrigal. (NS 6B)

(Extension) The student will perform or observe the addition of instrumental accompaniment to a madrigal-like vocal piece. (NS 2)

(Extension) The student will combine drama, poetry, dance, and music to create a Shakespearean scene. (NS 8A)

- Perform an SA, TB, or SATB song which includes intervals of a 2nd, 3rd, 4th, and 5th.

POSTURE/BREATH

1. Stretch overhead, side to side, up and down, then shake to relax any tight muscles.

2. Raise your arms overhead, stretching the fingers out in all directions. Bring the arms back to the sides, relaxed and free of tension.

3. Exhale all your air. Wait for a moment until your body lets you know it needs air. Allow the air to flow in without effort.

4. Sip air through a straw. Allow your lungs and rib cage to expand outward.

5. Place your fingertips just below your rib cage and take a "surprised" breath. Notice the movement of the diaphragm.

Tone
Review the 5 basic vowels used in choral singing: ee, eh, ah, oh, oo. Remember when you sing these vowels to sing with a relaxed jaw and vertical space inside the mouth.

ee   eh   ah   oh   oo

Quickly and detached

⑥

hah hah hah hah | hoh hoh hoh hoh | hah hah hah hah | hoh
hoo | hee | hoo | hee
hee | heh | hee | heh

TEACHING SUGGESTIONS

Essential Elements:
• The student will sing with tall uniform vowels. (NS 1A)
• The student will display the posture and breath control needed to support choral tone. (NS 1A)

Focus:
The principle of tall uniform vowels can be extended to all vowel sounds.

Teaching Tips:
• Teach student pages 87-88 in a single lesson.
• Review the five basic vowels.
• Sing Exercise 6, focusing on pure vowels.

TONE

There are many other vowel sounds used in both speaking and singing. Here are some examples of other vowel sounds. As a general rule: Sing the vowel sound as you would say it, but modify the vowel in the following ways:

- Keep a relaxed jaw
- Maintain vertical space inside the mouth
- Keep the corners of the mouth from spreading outward

Repeat ⑦ - ⑨ at different pitch levels

⑦
(ih) (ih) (ih) (ih)
Bring a gift of silk to the la - dy.

" ĭ " as in gift

⑧
(ă) (ă) (ă)
The cat sat in the hat.

" ă " as in cat

⑨
(ŭ) (ŭ)
Fun _____ in the sun

" ŭ " as in fun

Teaching Tips: *(continued)*

- *Present the information on this student page, stressing to students that English requires more than just the five basic vowel sounds.*
- *A general rule for singing vowel sounds is to modify the vowel in the ways described in the student text.*
- *Practice exercise 6 on page 87 with vowel sounds other than the 5 basic, pure vowels: ă, ĭ, ŭ.*
- *Exercises 7-9 allow practice of actual words instead of isolated vowels.*
- *Create exercises using words which are particular challenges in pieces you are performing.*

HARMONIC INTERVALS

Let's review intervals. In the last chapter we learned that an *interval* is the measurement between two pitches. When intervals are played in succession, they are called *melodic intervals*.

When intervals are played simultaneously, they are called *harmonic* intervals. Here are some examples of harmonic intervals.

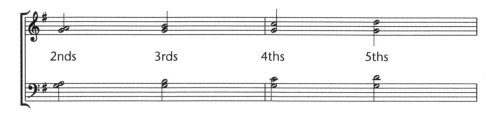

2nds   3rds   4ths   5ths

Harmonic intervals are the building blocks of harmony. Two or more harmonic intervals combined form a *chord*. Thus, a *chord* is the combination of 3 or more tones played simultaneously. Here are some examples of chords.

Check your knowledge!
1. What are intervals played simultaneously called?

2. What are intervals played in succession called?

3. What is a *chord*?

TEACHING SUGGESTIONS

Essential Elements:
• The student will recognize harmonic intervals. (NS 5E)

Focus:
Harmonic intervals are the building blocks of harmony.

Teaching Tips:
• Review melodic intervals.
• Define harmonic intervals.
• Illustrate harmonic intervals using the examples on this student page.
• Demonstrate at the piano if you wish.
• Answer the Check Your Knowledge! questions. (All the answers for Check Your Knowledge! are located on this page.)

Student
Book Page
90

PRACTICE WITH INTERVALS

Practice the following exercises. Notice the harmonic intervals that result when one group sustains a pitch while the other group moves to a higher or lower pitch. Listen carefully for balance, tuning, and blend.

Remember that a fermata (𝄐) means to hold a note (or rest) longer than its normal value.

Practice the following exercises in 3 parts. Notice the chord that results as one group sustains a pitch while 2 other groups move higher and lower.

"Don't get discouraged if your choir cannot sing these exercises in tune on the first attempt. Return to this page as needed or incorporate these exercises into your daily warm-up."

TEACHING SUGGESTIONS

Essential Elements:
• The student will recognize and perform harmonic intervals in an ensemble. (NS 5E)

Focus:
Students will experience singing harmonic intervals and chords.

Teaching Tips:
• Follow the procedures as presented on this page, listening carefully for intonation and balance.
• Alternate voice parts.
• Adapt these exercises as part of your daily routine.
• Transpose these exercises to help establish tonality before rehearsing a particular song.

MELODY AND HARMONY

Sing each line separately and in combination. Can you describe the time and key signature?

①

②

③

④

⑤

⑥

⑦

⑧

Teaching Tips: *(continued)*

- *Follow your procedures for sight-reading new material. See Teacher p. 75.*
- *Review time signatures with your students, emphasizing ¾ meter.*
- *Combine lines if the unison lines are secure.*
- *Emphasize the importance of establishing and maintaining a steady beat, particularly on lines which contain rests.*
- *All voices may sing all lines as you wish, but changing voices may have more success with Exercises 1, 3, 7, 8.*

TREBLE • TENOR BASS • MIXED

Musical Terms

> *accent*; emphasis on one note (or chord) over others around it. When singing a note that is accented, you can emphasize the note by singing it louder or by stressing the beginning consonant or vowel that starts the word. You can also use the diaphragm to create a breath accent.

accel. – accelerando; becoming faster; a gradual increase in tempo.

History: The author of this text, *Francis Beaumont*, was an English playwright who lived from c.1584-1616 and was a contemporary of William Shakespeare. It was quite common for plays of this period to use music.

Dance!
For SA, TB or SATB and Piano

Text by
FRANCIS BEAUMONT (1584-1616)

Music by
EMILY CROCKER

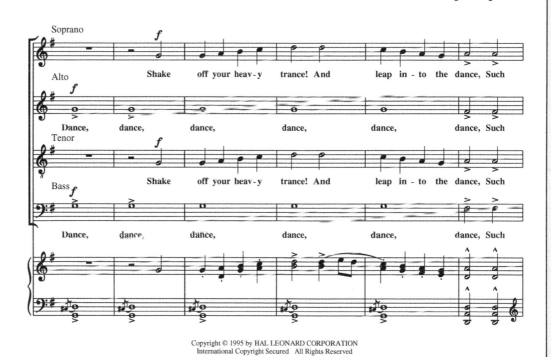

TEACHING SUGGES-TIONS

Essential Elements:
- The student will become familiar with the musical terms which appear on this page and in the song. (NS 5C)
- The student will apply music reading skills to an accompanied song in the key of G. (NS 5A, 5C)
- The student will recognize form through repetition and contrast of musical material. (NS 5D)

Focus:
Perform a song in parts which includes interval skips and varied style markings.

Teaching Tips:
- Read the text with your students. Explain that in mythology, Apollo was the god of music. In the period in which the poet lived, mythological themes were common and often occurred in musical or theatrical settings.
- Learn this piece using your established sight-reading procedure.
- Note that this song can be sung by treble (sing SA), tenor bass (sing TB) or mixed choirs (sing SATB).
- Review vowel sounds as presented on student page 88. Experiment with vowel modifications to create a pleasing choral tone on the word "dance." (NOTE: Be careful that you don't nasalize the word "dance".)

- Establish and maintain a steady beat while rehearsing the staggered entrances.
- Emphasize articulation, especially on the accented notes.
- Review and identify polyphonic and homophonic sections. See student page 47.
- Note that m. 5-14 and 16-21 are almost identical. Pointing out such similarities helps students begin to recognize form.
- Perform the entire piece, emphasizing stylistic markings.
- Note the accelerando at m. 23. This may need to be rehearsed carefully.

Essential Elements:
- (Extension) The student will discuss and analyze the characteristics of a madrigal. (NS 6B)
- (Extension) The student will perform or observe the addition of instrumental accompaniment to a madrigal-like vocal piece. (NS 2)
- (Extension) The student will combine drama, poetry, dance, and music to create a Shakespearean scene. (NS 8A)

Extension:
- *Play a recording of a madrigal, noting that this piece was written in dance-like madrigal style.*
- *Add instruments to "Dance." (strings, percussion, recorders, etc.)*
- *Perform "Dance" in a concert setting.*
- *Read poetry, or act out a scene from Shakespeare in which this song could have been used. Perform this song as a part of a scene for English classes in your school.*

EE 14: GOALS AND OVERVIEW

In this chapter, students are introduced to the concept of *word stress* through the use of the unstressed vowel called a *schwa*. This is a relatively sophisticated concept, and some groups may not be ready to effectively incorporate this concept into their singing. Stress to students that when they sing a musical phrase, the text must have a natural rise and fall, just as speaking does. Continue to sing with tall, uniform vowels, but also begin to incorporate this refinement, which will give the performance more expressiveness.

Also presented in this chapter is the concept of the *tonic chord*. The intervals of the tonic chord will be the first interval skips the students will experience in the following sight-reading and performance material. The ability to sing and identify the tonic chord is a vital skill for all musicians. Notice that the rhythmic demands are minimal, in order to allow the student to concentrate on the challenging new melodic concepts.

ESSENTIAL ELEMENTS AND NEW CONCEPTS

Voice:
The student will develop posture and breath control needed to support choral tone. (NS 1A)
The student will understand and practice the neutral vowel (schwa). (NS 1A)

- *Schwa*, unstressed words and syllables
- Importance of physical fitness for a singer

Theory:
The student will understand and be able to identify triad and tonic chord. (NS 5D)

- *Triad*
- *Tonic, tonic chord*
- Tonic chord melody drills and chord builders in the key of G

Sight-Reading:
The student will read and sing melodic patterns using the tonic chord. (NS 5B, 5C, 5E)

- Tonic chord practice in the key of G

Performance:
The student will identify and perform the musical terms and style markings in a short piece. (NS 5C)
The student will perform short songs which emphasize the tonic chord. (NS 1E)
(Extension) The student will relate a song based on the poetry of Christina Rossetti used in this song to other poetry examples. (NS 8B)
(Extension) The student will improvise a harmonic accompaniment to the reading of a Christina Rossetti poem using an autoharp or other chordal instrument. (NS 3A)
(Extension) The student will combine history, drama, and music in an in-class presentation. (NS 8A)

- Musical terms: *opt. div., ostinato, fine, ode*
- Perform SA, TB, and SATB songs in the key of G which include tonic chord melodic intervals.

POSTURE/BREATH

1. Stretch your arms overhead, then bend at the waist and stretch toward the floor. Slowly rise up, one vertebra at a time until you are in a standing posture.

2. Rotate your shoulders, first your left, then your right, then both shoulders. Raise your head so that it is in line with the spinal column, and not tilted up or down. Remember to stand in a good singing posture:
   • Stand with feet apart (Is your weight balanced?)
   • Knees unlocked (Can you bend them easily?)
   • Back straight (Are you standing erect comfortably and not stiff?)
   • Head erect (Is your chin level, and not too far up or down?)
   • Rib cage lifted (Is your chest high and able to expand?)
   • Shoulders relaxed (Are they comfortably down, not too far forward or back?)
   • Hands at your side (Are they relaxed and free of tension?)

3. When people are suddenly startled, they usually take a deep natural breath very quickly. Take a "surprised" breath. Notice the action of the diaphragm.

4. Imagine that there is an elevator platform at the bottom of your lungs. Drop the platform toward the floor as you inhale. Inhale 4 counts, exhale 4 counts. Repeat with 5, then 6 counts.

Physical Exercise: A regular program of physical exercise is very useful in a singer's development. Exercise improves breath capacity, the cardiovascular system, endurance, and general good health. Be sure to have a physician's approval before beginning any exercise program, but the benefits of such a program are significant.

Tone/Articulation
Review the following vowels: ĭ (gift), ă (cat), ŭ (run)

TEACHING SUGGESTIONS

Essential Elements:
• The student will develop posture and breath control needed to support choral tone. (NS 1A)
• The student will understand and practice the neutral vowel (schwa). (NS 1A)

Focus:
The neutral vowel (ə = schwa) is often used in an unstressed word or syllable.

Teaching Tips:
• Practice the exercises as presented on this page.
• This is a good time to relate the physical process of singing to physical exercise. Stress that singers who are physically fit usually have improved breath support and endurance.
• Review the short vowel sounds using the exercise on student page 95.

THE NEUTRAL VOWEL

The second syllable of the following words and several one-syllable words use what is called the neutral vowel (ə), also called *schwa*. It might be described as similar to an "uh" sound, and is an unstressed word or syllable. To produce this vowel:
- Keep space inside the mouth
- Maintain a vertical mouth shape
- Do not allow the corners of the mouth to spread outward
- The mouth is more closed than an "ah" vowel

Examples:

(ə)	(ə)	(ə)	(ə)	(ə)	(ə)	(ə)	(ə)
↓	↓	↓	↓	↓			↓
sofa	*nearest*	*quiet*	*autumn*	*joyous*	*of*	*the*	*wouldn't*

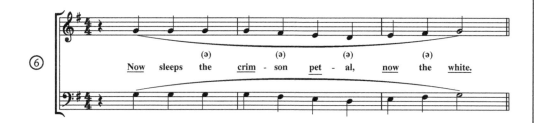

⑥ Now sleeps the crim - son pet - al, now the white.

⑦ Bas - kets of ro - ses we bring from the gar - den.

> "Word stress is a refinement in choral music, a detail which creates an even more polished performance."

Teaching Tips: *(continued)*

- *Introduce unstressed, neutral vowels as presented on this page, reminding students to keep space inside the mouth and to maintain a vertical mouth shape.*
- *Speak the neutral vowels as listed.*
- *Sing the neutral vowels.*
- *Compare the unstressed, neutral vowels on this page to the same vowel on a stressed syllable, i.e. "sofa" and "father."*

- *Perform exercises 6 & 7 on p. 96 using words which contain the neutral vowels. First speak the text, stressing the important words and then sing the text using the same word stress.*
- *Remind students to use neutral vowels on unstressed words or syllables.*

Extension:
- *Apply the concept of unstressed neutral vowels to music that the students are performing.*

TRIAD AND TONIC CHORD

Let's review chords. In the last chapter, we learned that two or more harmonic intervals combined form a *chord*. So, a *chord* is the combination of 3 or more tones played or sung simultaneously.

A *triad* is a special type of 3-note chord built in 3rds over a *root tone*. Following are some examples of triads.

Triads

When a *triad* is built on the key note of a major scale it is called a *tonic chord*. You'll notice that the word *tonic* is related to the word tone. *Tonic* is another way of referring to the keynote in a major scale and *tonic chord* is another way of referring to the triad built on that keynote.

Tonic chord: C major   Tonic chord: G major

Check your knowledge!

1. How many tones are needed to form a chord?

2. Describe a *triad*.

3. What is another name for keynote?

4. What tone of the major scale is a tonic chord built on?

5. Is the *tonic chord* a triad?

TEACHING SUGGESTIONS

Essential Elements:
• The student will understand and describe the concepts of triad and tonic chord. (NS 5D)

Focus:
A triad is a 3-note chord built in 3rds over a root tone. A triad built on the keynote of a major scale is a tonic chord.

Teaching Tips:
• Read and discuss the information presented on page 97, illustrating at the chalkboard and/or keyboard as necessary.
• If keyboards are available, invite students to play triads.
• Answers to Check Your Knowledge! are found within the text on this page.

Student Book Page **98**

TONIC CHORD PRACTICE

Practice the following drills which outline the tonic chord. Remember, when the melody utlines the tonic chord, you are singing melodic intervals. When 3 or more parts sing the pitches of the tonic chord simultaneously, the ensemble is singing a chord.

The Tonic Chord

Melody Drills

Chord Builders

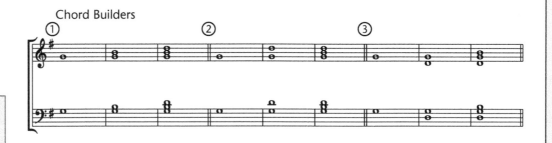

"Flatting happens! The third of the chord is often (always!) vulnerable. Tune patiently."

Teaching Tips: *(continued)*

• *Practice the melodic intervals of the G major tonic chord.*
• *Extend this practice using the Melody Drills on this page.*
• *Divide the choir by sections and perform the Chord Builders, listening carefully for intonation, balance and blend.*
• *Treble and tenor bass choirs can perform Chord Builders in three parts; mixed choirs may divide into six parts.*

Student
Book Page
99

MORE TONIC CHORD PRACTICE

Echo-sing each line or sing as a group, until the melodic patterns of the tonic chord are familiar.

① ②

④

⑤

TEACHING SUGGESTIONS

Essential Elements:

• The student will read and sing melodic patterns using the tonic chord. (NS 5B, 5C, 5E)

Focus:

Apply knowledge of triads and tonic chords to sight-reading.

Teaching Tips:

• Practice the tonic chords on student page 99 using your established method of sight-reading.

• Less experienced groups may require more drill to internalize the tonality of the tonic chord.

• Check intonation constantly.

• Apply expanded rib cage breathing and good vocal technique to help intonation.

TONIC CHORD EXERCISES

Sing each line separately and in any combination.

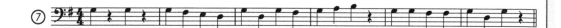

Teaching Tips: *(continued)*

- *These exercises are further practice of the tonic chord. Note that any line may be combined with any other exercise on this page.*
- *Sight-read each line separately; combine when unison lines are secure.*
- *Encourage all voices to sing all lines; changing voices may find more success with exercises 1, 4, 5, and 6. Changing voices may switch octaves or omit notes when exercises are out of range.*

TREBLE CHORUS

History: In this piece for treble chorus, the text is by Christina Rossetti, a 19th century English poet who lived in the Victorian era from 1830-1894. Rossetti, who has been described as one of the greatest poets of her time, wrote both of nature and of the spirit. Her brother, Dante Gabriel Rossetti, was also a well-known poet and painter.

Musical Terms:
opt. div. – optional *divisi*; the part splits into optional harmony. The smaller sized *cue notes* indicate the optional notes to be used.

As you prepare *Spring Quiet*, concentrate on the following:
• Notice the interval skips in the *tonic chord*.
• In measures 9 and 11, notice the quarter rest on the first beat of the measure.
• In measure 17, the melody is presented as a *canon*. In measure 21, notice how the melody outlines the *tonic chord*.
• Sing with full breath support and good vowels and articulation.
• If you sing the *opt. divisi*, notice the full 3-part tonic chord in the last measure.

Spring Quiet
For SA a cappella

CHRISTINA ROSSETTI (adapted)

Music by
EMILY CROCKER

TEACHING SUGGESTIONS

Essential Elements:
• The student will identify and perform the musical terms and style markings in a short piece. (NS 5C)
• The student will perform short songs which emphasize the tonic chord. (NS 1E)

Focus:
Apply knowledge of the tonic chord to the performance of a short a cappella song.

Teaching Tips:
• Read the information about the poet in the student text.
• Introduce the new musical term, opt. div.
• Refer to performance and teaching sequence suggestions for "Spring Quiet" included in the student text.
• Follow your established sight-reading procedure.
• Learn the rhythm and pitches prior to adding the text.
• Identify the stressed and unstressed words or syllables in the text by speaking the text before singing.

• Remind singers to use the neutral vowel (schwa) on unstressed words and syllables.
• The third and seventh scale degrees and all descending intervals may tend to flat. Tune them carefully.

Essential Elements:
- (Extension) The student will relate a song based on the poetry of Christina Rossetti used in this song to other poetry examples. (NS 8B)
- (Extension) The student will improvise a harmonic accompaniment to the reading of a Christina Rossetti poem using an autoharp or other chordal instrument. (NS 3A)

Teaching Tips: (continued)

- Tune the third of the final chord carefully.
- Note that tenor bass choirs may sing "Spring Quiet" one octave lower.

Extension:
- Review the information about the poet Christina Rossetti on student page 101.
- Suggest students find other poetry by Christina Rossetti and share them with the class. Accompany the reading of the poetry with an improvised accompaniment on an autoharp or other chordal instrument.
- Encourage interested students to compose a song using a Rossetti text.

TENOR BASS CHORUS

History: In music during the 16th century, an *ode* was a text set to music in a strict chordal style and in a rhythm dictated by the rhythm of the words of the poem.

The text for the piece that follows, *Sons of Art*, while contemporary, has similarities to the odes of an earlier time.

Henry Purcell (1659-1695) was an English composer of the Baroque Period who wrote odes and hundreds of other songs, choral pieces, instrumental and dramatic works. As a composer for the English court, in 1694 he wrote a famous ode on the occasion of Queen Mary II's birthday entitled *Come Ye Sons of Art, Away.*

Musical Terms:

ostinato – a repeated pattern. Notice how the bass part in this piece repeats the same four bars. This serves as an accompaniment device beneath the tenor melody.

opt. div. – optional *divisi*; the part splits into optional harmony. The smaller sized *cue notes* indicate the optional notes to be used.

fine – an Italian term for *end*. After a repeat the *fine* sign indicates the end of the piece.

As you prepare *Sons of Art*:
• Use good breath support, vowels, and articulation.
• Sing musically
• If you sing the *opt. divisi* at the end, notice the full 3-part tonic chord in the last measure.

Sons of Art
For TB a cappella

Words and Music by
EMILY CROCKER

Teaching Tips:

• Read the History information in the student text.
• Introduce the new musical terms: ostinato, opt. div. and fine.
• Refer to performance and teaching sequence suggestions for "Sons of Art" in the student text.
• Follow your established sight-reading procedure.
• Make sure rhythm and pitch are secure before adding the text.
• Identify the stressed and unstressed words or syllables in the text by speaking the text before singing.

• Remind singers to use the neutral vowel (schwa) on unstressed words and syllables.
• The third and seventh scale degrees and all descending intervals may tend to flat. Tune them carefully.

TENOR BASS

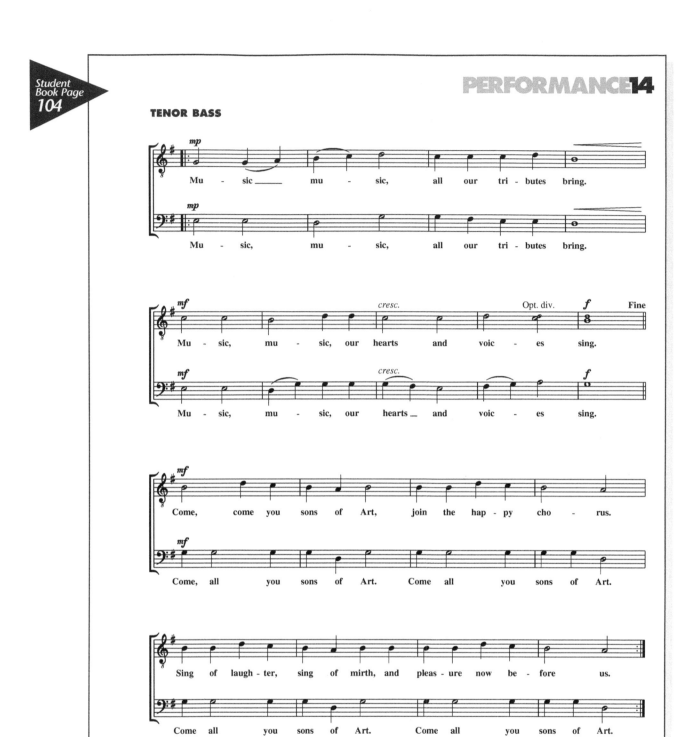

Teaching Tips: (continued)

• Note that treble choirs may sing "Sons Of Art"
  one octave higher.

Extension:
• Review the information about the composer Henry
  Purcell on student page 103.
• Play a recording of the Purcell version of "Come
  Ye Sons Of Art".

Student Book Page 105

MIXED CHORUS

History: In the early stages of America's nationhood, the purpose of education was aimed at practical and religious matters. Music for worship and recreation was primarily an oral tradition – people learned music by listening to it.

As time passed, however, the quality of singing declined so that a clergyman of the time wrote: "The tunes are now miserably tortured and twisted... into a horrid medley of confused and disordered voices."

In response to these concerns, *Singing Schools* developed. These singing schools were led by traveling teachers who for a fee would teach the basics of reading music in small towns and villages. Sometimes whole families would attend, and enjoyed the social aspect of singing together in a group.

Music became a part of the school curriculum for the first time in 1838 when *Lowell Mason* convinced the Boston School Committee to include it in the public schools.

Lowell Mason wrote many songs and choral pieces during his lifetime, including the text for the piece that follows.

As you prepare to sing *O Music, Sweet Music*:
• Notice how the melody outlines the tonic chord.
• When all three parts combine, listen as the 3-parts create harmony.
• In measure 9, the melody is restated, this time as a 3-part canon.
• Sing with good breath support, vowels, and articulation.

O Music, Sweet Music

For SATB a cappella

Words by LOWELL MASON
Music by JOHN LEAVITT

Teaching Tips: *(continued)*

• *Refer to performance and teaching sequence suggestions for "O Music, Sweet Music" in the student text.*
• *Follow your established sight-reading procedure.*
• *Make sure that rhythm and pitch are secure before adding the text.*
• *Identify the stressed and unstressed words or syllables in the text by speaking the text before singing.*

• *Remind singers to use the neutral vowel (schwa) on unstressed words and syllables.*
• *The third and seventh scale degrees and all descending intervals may tend to flat. Tune them carefully.*

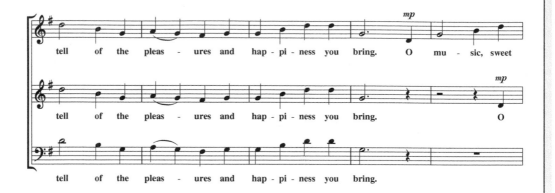

tell of the pleas - ures and hap - pi - ness you bring. O mu - sic, sweet

tell of the pleas - ures and hap - pi - ness you bring. O

tell of the pleas - ures and hap - pi - ness you bring.

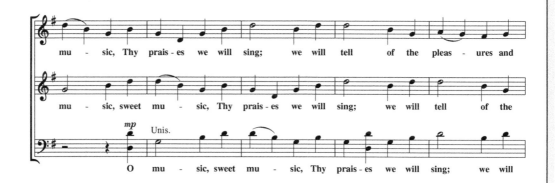

mu - sic, Thy prais - es we will sing; we will tell of the pleas - ures and

mu - sic, sweet mu - sic, Thy prais - es we will sing; we will tell of the

O mu - sic, sweet mu - sic, Thy prais - es we will sing; we will

hap - pi - ness you bring.

pleas - ures and hap - pi - ness you bring.

tell of the pleas - ures and hap - pi - ness you bring.

Essential Elements:
- (Extension) The student will combine history, drama and music in an in-class presentation. (NS 8A)

Teaching Tips: (continued)

- Note that treble and tenor bass choirs may sing this canon. Notes out of range may be sung in a more comfortable octave.
- Check for balance among the three parts of the canon.

Extension:
- Review the information about the composer and music educator Lowell Mason and Singing Schools on student page 105.
- Discover how learning to read music has changed since the time of the Singing Schools. **Music Education in the United States** by Henry Bailey Birge is a source for this information. (See Bibliography on page 203.)
- Encourage a group of students to act out a typical singing school lesson from the time of Lowell Mason, using the song "O Music, Sweet Music" as part of the skit.

EE 15: GOALS AND OVERVIEW

This chapter reviews and practices the material covered up to this point. It also includes three longer, accompanied songs which may be used for both sight-reading practice and concert performance.

Use this opportunity to assess your students' musical progress in large group, small group, or on an individual basis.

ESSENTIAL ELEMENTS AND NEW CONCEPTS

Voice:
The student will review the posture, breathing, vowel placement and articulation necessary for good choral tone. (NS 1A)
The student will review the vocal mechanism. (NS 1A)

• Review Chapters 1-14.

Theory:
The student will review intervals, chords and triads. (NS 5D)

• Review Chapters 12-14.

Sight-Reading:
The student will sight-read exercises which emphasize the tonic chord and "pickup notes." (NS 5E)

• "Pickup" notes
• Practice sight-reading melodies in the key of G which include tonic chord melodic intervals.
• Combinable exercises

Performance:
The student will identify and perform the musical terms and style markings in these pieces. (NS 5C)
The student will perform songs emphasizing the tonic chord. (NS 1E)
(Extension) The student will relate music performed in class with events in American history. (NS 8B)
(Extension) The student will combine dance and music for an in-class presentation. (NS 8A)

• Sing SA, TB, and SATB songs in the key of G major which include tonic chord melodic intervals.

REVIEW AND PRACTICE

1. Describe the steps for a good singing posture.

2. How does an expanded rib cage affect breath capacity?

3. What are the five basic vowel sounds? Describe the basic formation of each.

4. What is the general rule for producing other vowel sounds in addition to the five basic vowel sounds?

5. What is the *neutral vowel*?

6. Describe the difference in the vowel sounds of the following:
    *   2nd syllable of *sofa*
    *   1st syllable of *father*

7. What is *articulation* in singing? What are the three main *articulators*?

8. What is the source of vocal tone? What is it popularly called?

9. How do the vocal folds produce sound?

10. How can physical exercise help to improve singing?

Tone/Articulation
Sing the following exercise which reviews vowel shape and articulation. Repeat at different pitch levels.

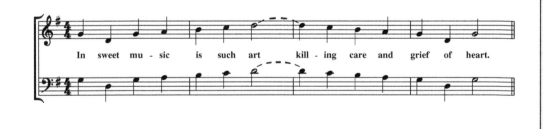

In sweet mu-sic is such art kill-ing care and grief of heart.

TEACHING SUGGESTIONS

Essential Elements:
*   The student will review the posture, breathing, vowel placement and articulation necessary for good choral tone. (NS 1A)
*   The student will review the vocal mechanism. (NS 1A)

Focus:
Review and apply information learned in chapters 1-14.

Teaching Tips:
*   Answer the questions in large group or coopera-tive learning situations.

Answers: (Page numbers refer to the student text.)
1. The steps for good singing are: stand with feet apart, knees unlocked, back straight, head erect, rib cage lifted, shoulders relaxed, hands at your side. (p. 1)
2. An expanded rib cage increases breath capacity. (p. 1)
3. The five basic vowels sounds are "ee, eh, ah, oh, oo". The basic formation is: a relaxed jaw, space inside the mouth, and a vertical mouth shape. (p. 5)

4. The general rule for producing other vowel sounds in addition to the five basic vowels: sing the vowel as you would say it, but modify the vowel by keeping a relaxed jaw, maintaining vertical space in the mouth, keeping the corners of the mouth from spreading outward. (p. 88).
5. A neutral vowel is also called schwa and refers to an "uh" sound on an unstressed word or syllable. (p. 96).
6. The second syllable of "sofa" is an unstressed neutral vowel and the first syllable of "father" is a stressed "ah" vowel. (p. 96)
7. Articulation is the pronunciation of the conso-nants. The three main articulators are the lips, teeth and tongue. (p. 52).

8. The source of vocal tone is the larynx. It is popularly called the voice box. (p. 80)
9. The vocal folds produce sound by vibrating. Exhaled air passes between the vocal cords causing them to vibrate. (p. 80)
10. Physical exercise helps to improve singing by improving breath capacity, cardiovascular system, endurance and general good health. (p. 95)

*   Ask students to apply their knowledge and skill in the performance of the exercise on student p. 107. Identify the words which include the basic vowel sounds. Are there any neutral vowels? (Yes, "of").

REVIEW AND PRACTICE

Check your knowledge!

1. What is an *interval*?

2. What is the difference between *melodic* and *harmonic* intervals?

3. What is a *chord*?

4. How many tones are needed to form a chord?

5. What is the difference between a *chord* and a *triad*?

6. What is another name for *keynote*?

7. What tone of the major scale is a *tonic chord* built on?

8. Is the tonic chord a triad?

Identify the following melodic and harmonic intervals.

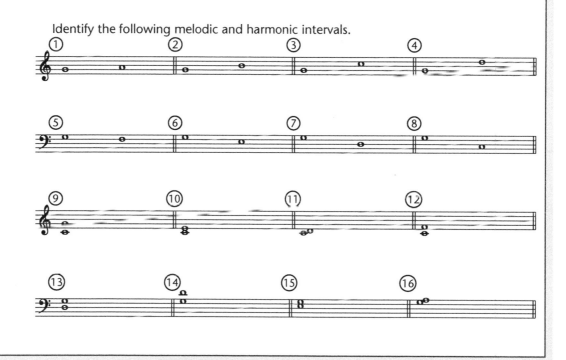

TEACHING SUGGESTIONS

Essential Elements:
• The student will review intervals, chords and triads. (NS 5D)

Focus:
Review theory information in chapters 12-14.

Teaching Tips:
• Answer Check Your Knowledge! questions in large group or cooperative learning situations.

Answers: (Page numbers refer to the student text.)
1. An interval is a measurement between two pitches. (p. 81)
2. Melodic intervals are intervals sounded in succession. (p. 81) Harmonic intervals are intervals which are sounded simultaneously. (p. 89)
3. A chord is two or more harmonic intervals combined. (p. 89)
4. Three or more tones are needed to form a chord. (p. 89)

5. A chord is the combination of three or more tones played or sung simultaneously. A triad is a three-note chord built in thirds over a root tone. (p. 97)
6. Another name for keynote is tonic. (p. 97)
7. A tonic chord is built on the keynote or tonic. (p. 97)
8. Yes. It is a triad built on the keynote or tonic. (p. 97)

Answers to Interval Identification:
1=2nd, 2=3rd, 3=4th, 4=5th, 5=2nd, 6=3rd, 7=4th, 8=5th, 9=5th, 10=3rd, 11=2nd, 12=4th, 13=4th, 14=5th, 15=3rd, 16=2nd

TONIC CHORD • PICKUP NOTE

Musical Terms:

pickup note(s) – A pickup note(s) (also called *upbeat* or *anacrusis*) is one or more notes which occur before the first barline.

Sing each line separately and in any combination. Notice the *pickup note* in each exercise.

TEACHING SUGGESTIONS

Essential Elements:

• The student will sight-read exercises which emphasize the tonic chord and "pickup notes." (NS 5E)

Focus:

Pickup notes are one or more notes which occur before the first barline.

Teaching Tips:

• All of these exercises are extracted from the performance songs in this chapter. (student p. 111-117)

• Introduce the concept of pick-up notes. Note that contemporary editorial practice no longer shortens the final measure of a song when a pick-up occurs at the beginning. However, in older editions, the last bar is correspondingly shortened.

• Follow your established procedure for sight-reading new material.

• Combine lines as ready.

• Encourage all voices to sing all lines. Changing voices may switch octaves or omit notes when pitches are out of range. Changing voices may be most successful on lines 4 and 5. New baritones will be most successful with lines 6, 7, and 8.

Student
Book Page
110

KING WILLIAM
Treble Chorus • Tenor Bass Chorus

History: The text for *King William* is taken from an Early American *Play-Party* song. Play-parties were social events at which young people came together for refreshments, games, and singing. In many communities of the time, dancing was frowned upon, and while the play parties included ring dances, reels, and other partner games, the participants sang the songs without instrumental accompaniment, and so they were considered to be games or "play-parties" rather than actual dances.

In this play-party song, a young man would stand holding a broad-brimmed hat in his hand. Then he would place the hat on a girl's head, and they marched together, linking arms. At the end of the song, the girl placed the hat on another boy's head, and they continued as before. The song was repeated until all had a turn. At each "crowning" of the hat the couple would exchange a kiss.

As you prepare to perform *King William*:
• Find the places where the melody outlines the tonic chord. Practice these intervals so that you can sing them accurately.
• Read the rhythm, add the pitches, and repeat until accurate.
• Sing with good breath support and articulation.
• Identify the *neutral vowels* in the text and sing them with less stress:
  <u>Will</u>-iam   <u>Georg</u>-es, etc.

HOSANNA
Mixed Chorus

History: The word *Hosanna* (or *Osanna*) is a Hebrew word expressing triumph and glory. The phrase *Hosanna in excelsis Deo* is a phrase taken from the *Sanctus*, a section of the Latin mass. Since the advent of polyphony in music, the *Hosanna* has often been set to exciting music in a brilliant style. The *Hosanna* is often presented as a *coda* or ending section of the *Sanctus*.

As you prepare to perform *Hosanna*:
• Notice where the melody outlines the intervals of the tonic chord. Practice these sections so that you can sing them accurately.
• Notice how the parts enter in a staggered pattern, but not as in a canon. Rather, the entrances can be described as *imitative*, because they imitate each other, but not exactly.
• Read the rhythm, add the pitches, and repeat as necessary for accuracy.
• Pronounce the Latin phrases: *aw-SAH-nah een ek-SHEL-sees DEH-awh, Ah-leh-LOO-ee-ah.*
• Sing the last syllable of *Ho-san-na* as a neutral vowel.

TEACHING SUGGESTIONS

Essential Elements:
• *The student will identify and perform the musical terms and style markings in these pieces. (NS 5C)*
• *The student will perform songs emphasizing the tonic chord. (NS 1E)*

Focus:
Apply knowledge of pickup notes and the tonic chord to the performance of a song.

Teaching Tips:
• *Note that treble and tenor bass choirs sing the same song written in appropriate notation. The treble version of "King William" appears on p. 111, and tenor bass is on student p. 113.*
• *Treble and tenor bass choruses may read the information about "King William" on this page as an introduction to the song.*
• *Mixed choruses may read the information about "Hosanna" on this page as an introduction to the song on student page 115.*

PERFORMANCE 15

TREBLE CHORUS

King William

For SA and Piano

Traditional text, adapted

Music by
EMILY CROCKER

Teaching Tips: *(continued)*

- *Sight-read "King William" for treble choir using your established method of sight-reading.*
- *Use the teaching suggestions on student p. 110 for learning this song.*
- *Practice and perform, paying special attention to word stress and tuning tonic chord intervals.*

Essential Elements:
- (Extension) The student will relate music performed in class with events in American history. (NS 8B)
- (Extension) The student will combine dance and music for an in-class presentation. (NS 8A)

Extension:
- Research information about early American play party songs and other aspects of Colonial and pre-Civil War American social life.

- Perform early American dances, using "King William" or other appropriate music.

TENOR BASS CHORUS

King William

For TB and Piano

Traditional text, adapted

Music by
EMILY CROCKER

Quickly (♩ = ca. 152)

Tenor

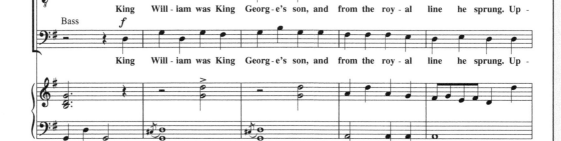

King Will - iam was King Georg - e's son, and from the roy - al line he sprung. Up -

Bass

King Will - iam was King Georg - e's son, and from the roy - al line he sprung. Up -

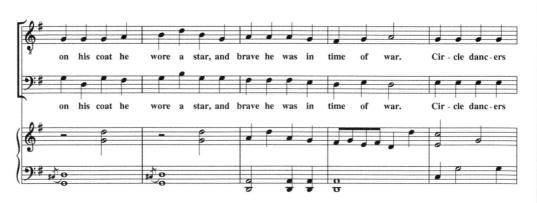

on his coat he wore a star, and brave he was in time of war. Cir - cle danc - ers

on his coat he wore a star, and brave he was in time of war. Cir - cle danc - ers

Teaching Tips: *(continued)*

- *Sight-read "King William" for tenor bass choir using your established method.*
- *Use the teaching suggestions on student p. 110 for learning this song.*
- *Practice and perform, paying special attention to word stress and tuning intervals in the tonic.*

Essential Elements:
- (Extension) The student will relate music performed in class with events in American history. (NS 8B)
- (Extension) The student will combine dance and music for an in-class presentation. (NS 8A)

Extension:
- Research information about early American play party songs and other aspects of Colonial and pre-Civil War American social life.

- Perform early American dances using "King William" or other appropriate music.

MIXED CHORUS

Hosanna

For SATB and Piano

Music by
JOHN LEAVITT

Teaching Tips: *(continued)*

- *Sight-read "Hosanna" for mixed choir using your established method.*
- *Use the teaching suggestions on student p. 110 for learning this song.*
- *Practice and perform, paying special attention to word stress and tuning tonic chord intervals.*
- *Pay special attention to accuracy on the pickups at the staggered entrances.*

Teaching Tips: *(continued)*

Extension:

• *Emphasize that "Hosanna" is a popular choral text which has been set by many composers throughout history. Play other examples such as the "Hosanna" from Bach's **B Minor Mass**.*

EE16: GOALS AND OVERVIEW

In this chapter, students are introduced to the key of F major by applying their knowledge of scale and key from previous chapters. If this information is well-learned, the students should have no difficulty in grasping these new concepts intellectually. In practical application, however, they will need to transfer their music-reading skills to a new key center, and this may take some practice. Notice that the melodic and rhythmic demands are not particularly challenging, to allow the students to experience success relatively quickly.

Also, this chapter introduces the concept of singing *diphthongs*, another vocal refinement which improves tone quality, blend, and intonation. The students should begin to listen critically to all the music they are performing, and assess their execution of this important vocal concept.

ESSENTIAL ELEMENTS AND NEW CONCEPTS

Voice:
The student will develop the posture and breath control needed to support choral tone. (NS 1A)
The student will understand and practice the appropriate pronunciation of diphthongs. (NS 1A)

- *Diphthongs*

Theory:
The student will understand and apply the concept of key signatures in the key of F major. (NS 5C, 5D)
The student will recognize and interpret the notation of dotted half notes. (NS 5C, 5D)

- Key of F
- Dotted half notes

Sight-Reading:
The student will practice singing chord patterns in the key of F major. (NS 5B, 5E)
The student will perform dotted half note notation. (NS 5C, 5D)

- Key of F practice
- Dotted half note practice
- Combinable exercises in the key of F

Performance:
The student will review the style markings which appear in the songs which follow. (NS 5C)
The student will apply music reading skills to the performance of a short song in the key of F major. (NS 5A, 5B, 5E)

- SA, TB, and SATB songs in the key of F, and in $\frac{3}{4}$ meter, allow students to apply musical concepts presented in this and previous chapters.

POSTURE/BREATH/TONE

1. Stretch, then yawn-sigh.

2. As you stand in your best singing posture, concentrate on relaxing and releasing the tension in your body without slumping.
   • Relax your neck and move your head forward and up, so that it is aligned with your spine.
   • Allow your spinal column to lengthen vertically.
   • Balance your weight evenly between your feet, and evenly between the heel and the ball of the feet.
   • Release the tension in your knees.
   • Release the tension in your shoulders.

3. Inhale with your mouth in an "ah" shape while pulling your elbows back. Bring your arms forward as you exhale on a whispered "oo." Repeat several times.

4. Imagine a milkshake as large as the room. "Drink" the air through a large straw.

Diphthongs (pronounced *DIF-thongs*)
You are familiar with the five basic vowels for choral singing: ee, eh, ah, oh, oo. As covered in previous chapters, other vowel sounds (ă, ŭ, ĭ, ə and others) are modifications of these basic vowels. A combination of two vowel sounds is called a *diphthong*. Since vowels are the basis of a free and open tone, and a choral sound that is blended and in tune, it is important to learn to sing vowels and diphthongs as an ensemble.

A diphthong consists of two vowel sounds: the *primary* vowel sound and a *secondary* vowel sound. This secondary vowel sound is (usually) at the very end of the diphthong, just before the final consonant or next word or syllable.

For example, the word "I" is really a diphthong using an "ah" and an "ee." The "ee" is a very brief, almost phantom sound at the end of the word.

I = ah _____ (ee)

ah   ee

TEACHING SUGGESTIONS

Essential Elements:
• The student will develop the posture and breath control needed to support choral tone. (NS 1A)
• The student will understand and practice the appropriate pronunciation of diphthongs. (NS 1A)

Focus:
Diphthongs consist of two vowel sounds. Emphasize the primary vowel when singing diphthongs.

Teaching Tips:
• Present the information about diphthongs on student p. 118 covering all points and demonstrating thoroughly.
• Imitate the illustrations on p. 118.

DIPHTHONGS

Here are some other common diphthongs. Sing each word on a unison pitch, and concentrate on maintaining the pure, primary vowel sound. Just as you release, place the final secondary vowel sound at the end of the tone. It should be very understated and unstressed. Can you think of other examples? Can you find examples in the music you are rehearsing?

day = (d)eh _____ (ee)

joy = (j)aw _____ (ee)

though = (th)oh _____ (oo)

Some diphthongs are formed from consonant sounds, and the secondary sound occurs before the primary vowel sound:

you = (ee)oo _____

want = (oo)ah _ _____ (nt)

Practice the following exercises using diphthongs.

Repeat with:

youth (ee-<u>oo</u>-th)
wise (oo-<u>ah</u>-ee-z)

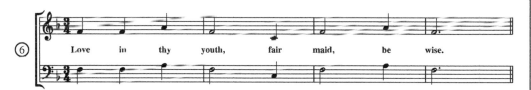

Teaching Tips: (continued)

- *Practice speaking and singing common diphthongs such as those on student p. 119.*
- *If students are having difficulty placing the secondary vowel appropriately on a word such as "day" [(d)eh-ee.], ask them to sing the word "date" and sing the "t" when you direct them. Then ask them to sing the secondary vowel "ee" in place of the "t". Practice this several times.*
- *After the singers can speak diphthongs correctly, ask them to sing words which contain diphthongs such as in exercises 5 and 6.*

Student Book Page *120*

DIPHTHONG PRACTICE

⑦

Now _____ *A - dieu.
nah _____ (oo) ah - d(ee)oo

Repeat with

my (m - <u>ah</u> - ee)
I (<u>ah</u> - ee)

* French for "good-bye"

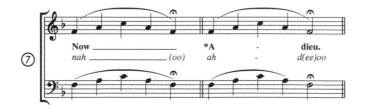

⑧

Now un - to my la - dy

⑨

my _____
mah _____ (ee)

Repeat with

way (oo - <u>eh</u> - ee)
life (I - <u>ah</u> - ee -f)

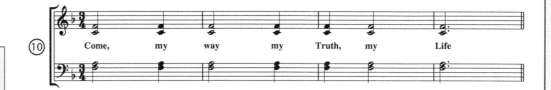

⑩

Come, my way my Truth, my Life

Good choral tone depends on the ability to sing vowels and diphthongs as an ensemble. Remember "You don't dance like you walk, and you don't sing like you talk."

Teaching Tips: *(continued)*

• *Practice diphthongs with precision, using the exercises on student p. 120.*

Extension:

• *Ask students to identify and practice the diphthongs in the songs which follow in this chapter and in other music which they are rehearsing.*

THEORY BUILDERS **16**

KEY OF F • DOTTED HALF NOTES

Key of F Major
The key of F major indicates that the keynote will be F. The grand staff below shows the F major scale as well as the whole/half step progression that is required for a major scale.

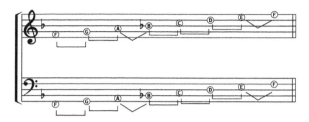
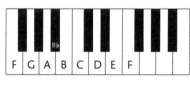

= whole step

= half step

This time, the whole/half step progression requires a B flat. (Remember that a flat lowers a pitch by one half step.) If we had written A-B, the interval between these two pitches would have been a whole step rather than the required half step.

Remember also that a key signature is placed after the clef sign at the beginning of a line. This time the flat is on B's line, and indicates that every time B occurs in the music, it should be sung as a B flat.

Dotted half notes
In our music notation, we need to be able to measure note values with durations of three beats (especially in meters of 3). Our notational system accomplishes this by adding a dot to the right of a note head. The rule governing dotted notes is the dot receives *half the value of the note to which it is attached.*

$\frac{3}{4}$ 𝅗𝅥 = 2 beats $\frac{3}{4}$ 𝅗𝅥. = 3 beats

Check your knowledge!
1. What is the key signature for the key of F major?

2. What is the dotted note rule?

3. How many beats does a half note receive in $\frac{3}{4}$ meter? A dotted half note?

TEACHING SUGGESTIONS

Essential Elements:
- The student will understand and apply the concept of key signatures in the key of F major. (NS 5C, 5D)
- The student will recognize and interpret the notation of dotted half notes. (NS 5C, 5D)

Focus:
Transfer knowledge of key signatures to the key of F major.

Teaching Tips:
- Review the whole/half step progression required for a major scale.
- Adapt that progression with F as the keynote, following the information presented on student p. 121.
- Stress that a flat will appear in the key signature and that all B notes will become B flat.
- Present this information using chalkboard or keyboard as appropriate.
- Explain dotted half note notation as presented on student p. 121.

- If students need more preparation for reading the exercises on student p. 124, teachers may want to design a rhythm drill using dotted half notes, or see the Appendix for additional rhythm drills. (Teacher p. 189)
- Review the information by discussing the Check Your Knowledge! questions. All answers may be found within the text on this page.

KEY OF F • DOTTED HALF NOTES

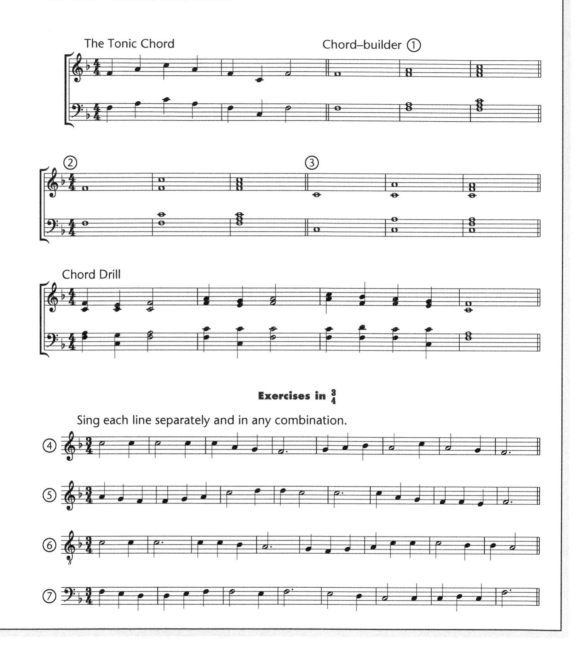

Exercises in ¾

Sing each line separately and in any combination.

TEACHING SUGGESTIONS

Essential Elements:
• The student will practice singing chord patterns in the key of F major. (NS 5B, 5E)
• The student will perform dotted half note notation. (NS 5C, 5D)

Focus:
Apply knowledge of F major and dotted half notes to sight-read melodic and harmonic exercises.

Teaching Tips:
• Sight-read student p. 122 using your established sight-reading procedure.
• After learning the Tonic Chord, Chord-Builder and Chord Drill exercises, consider using them as part of your daily warm-ups.
• Adapt the chord drill as needed for use with treble and tenor bass choirs.
• Sight-read exercises 4-7; combine when ready.
• Changing voices may find more success with 4 and 6. Encourage all voices to sing all parts.
• Notice that all exercises do not start on the keynote F, so you will need to establish the starting pitch of each line before singing.

Student Book Page
123

MORE PRACTICE

Sing each exercise separately and in any combination.

①

②

③

④

⑤

⑥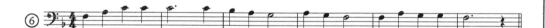

⑦

⑧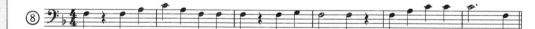

"Always encourage students to sing musically, even when sight-reading."

Teaching Tips: *(continued)*

- *This page provides additional drill and practice with dotted half notes in the key of F major.*
- *Sight-read, using your established sightreading procedures.*

LOVE IN THY YOUTH
Treble Chorus

History: In the 1600's, kings and other noblemen often hired musicians to work in their courts. One popular type of courtly music was the lute song. These songs, usually about love, were accompanied by the *lute*, an instrument similar to the guitar. The text of *Love in Thy Youth* was probably used for a lute song in a nobleman's court.

As you prepare to perform *Love In Thy Youth*:
• Look through the song and become familiar with the key of F major.
• Notice the places where the melody outlines the intervals of the tonic chord.
• Find the section of the song that is monophonic (unison melody). Find the section that is homophonic (parts that share the same or nearly the same rhythm, but on different pitches). Find the section that is polyphonic (parts have different rhythms).
• Read the rhythm, then add the pitch, and repeat as needed.
• Add the text and sing musically using good vowels, diphthongs, and articulation.

AS THE HOLLY GROWETH GREEN
Tenor Bass Chorus

History: Like the song for treble chorus described above, this song for tenor bass chorus *As the Holly Groweth Green* was probably a *lute* song. Sometimes kings would write their own texts or songs for their musicians to perform. King Henry VIII of England wrote the text of *As the Holly Groweth Green*.

As you prepare to sing *As The Holly Groweth Green*:
• Look through the song to become familiar with the key of F major.
• Find the places where the melody outlines the intervals of the tonic chord.
• Notice the call-response between the tenor and bass, in measure 43 on "adieu" (pronounced ah-d(ee)oo, the French word for "good-bye").
• Read the rhythm, add the pitch, repeat as needed.
• Add the text and sing musically, using good vowels, diphthongs, and articulation.

TEACHING SUGGESTIONS

Essential Elements:
• *The student will review the style markings which appear in the songs which follow. (NS 5C)*
• *The student will apply music reading skills to the performance of a short song in the key of F major. (NS 5A, 5B, 5E)*

Focus:
Transfer notation and diction skills to the performance of a short song.

Teaching Tips:
• *Note that in this Performance section, treble choirs will sing "Love In Thy Youth" student p. 125, tenor bass choirs will sing "As The Holly Groweth Green," student p. 127, and mixed choirs will sing "The Call," student p. 129.*
• *Read the information on this page as a preparation for sight-reading and performance.*

TREBLE CHORUS

Love In Thy Youth

For SA a cappella

Anonymous, 17th Century

Music by
EMILY CROCKER

Teaching Tips: *(continued)*

- Ask students to read the information on student
  p. 124 regarding the historical background for
  "Love In Thy Youth."
- Sight-read "Love In Thy Youth" using your established sight-reading procedures.
- Follow the performance suggestions as presented
  on student p. 124.
- Ask students to identify words in the text to "Love
  In Thy Youth" which contain diphthongs. If necessary, review diphthongs on student p. 118-
  120. Sing the diphthongs correctly.

Teaching Tips: *(continued)*

- *Take special note of words containing diphthongs which are slurred or change pitch as in the word "I" four measures from the end. Remind students that the secondary vowel sound should still be sung at the very end of the diphthong, not when the pitch changes.*
- *Note the optional divisi into three parts in the last three measures. Tune these chords carefully.*

Extension:

- *Play recordings of Renaissance lute music for the class.*

TENOR BASS CHORUS

As the Holly Groweth Green

For TB a cappella

KING HENRY VIII

Music by
EMILY CROCKER

Teaching Tips: (continued)

- Ask students to read the information on student p. 124 regarding the historical background on "As The Holly Groweth Green".
- Sight-read "As The Holly Groweth Green" using your established sight-reading procedures.
- Follow the performance suggestions as presented on student p. 124.
- Ask students to identify words in the text to "As The Holly Groweth Green" which contain diphthongs. If necessary, review diphthongs on student p. 118-120. Sing the diphthongs correctly.

Teaching Tips: *(continued)*

- *Notice the call and response between the tenor and bass on "adieu."*
- *"Adieu" is pronounced ah-d(ee)-oo with "oo" being the primary vowel.*

Extension:

- *Play recordings of Renaissance lute music for the class.*
- *Research information about the life of King Henry VIII.*

MIXED CHORUS

Musical Terms:

 First and second endings. A repeated section; the first time, sing the first ending; the second time, skip the first ending and go to the second ending.

As you prepare to perform *The Call*:
- Find the places where there is an interval skip in the F major tonic chord.
- Notice the quarter rest on the first beat of each phrase.
- Add the text and sing musically, using good vowels, diphthongs, and articulation.

The Call
For SATB a cappella

Words by GEORGE HERBERT (1593-1633)

Music by JOHN LEAVITT

Teaching Tips: *(continued)*

- *Familiarize students with first and second endings as suggested on student p. 129.*
- *Sight-read "The Call" using your established sight-reading procedures.*
- *Follow the performance suggestions as presented on student p. 129.*
- *Ask students to identify words in the text to "The Call" which contain diphthongs. If necessary, review diphthongs on student p. 118-120. Sing the diphthongs correctly.*
- *Remind students to hold the primary vowel of a diphthong for the full duration of the note before moving to the secondary vowel.*

EE17: GOALS AND OVERVIEW

This chapter presents the concept of eighth note and rest rhythms. In simple meter, where the quarter note receives the beat, the eighth note may be described as a *division* of the beat. Performing the eighth note division accurately is vital to maintaining the steady beat. Concentrate on this concept in all rhythm reading.

Also, students are presented with another aspect of articulation, the accurate and precise enunciation of "t" and "d". Transfer this knowledge to all music being performed, and encourage students to listen critically to their performance.

ESSENTIAL ELEMENTS AND NEW CONCEPTS

Voice:
The student will develop good diction through the articulation of consonants. (NS 1A)

- Clear diction using "t" and "d"

Theory:
The student will recognize and apply eighth note rhythm notation. (NS 5C, 5D)

- Eighth notes and rests
- Eighth note rhythm practice

Sight-Reading:
The student will read and perform rhythm patterns of eighth notes and rests accurately. (NS 5A)
(Extension) The student will compose short rhythm compositions. (NS 4A)
(Extension) The student will improvise short melodies over repeated rhythm patterns played on rhythm instruments. (NS 3C)

- Eighth note rhythm practice

Performance:
The student will combine text and rhythm. (NS 1E)
(Extension) The student will arrange a nursery rhyme or other poem for speech chorus. (NS 4B)

- Perform a 2-part speech chorus which uses eighth notes and rests.

POSTURE/BREATH

1. Stand in your best singing posture. Imagine there is a balloon attached to the top of your head. Allow the balloon to bring your head into alignment with your spine.

2. Exhale your air on an "ss" like air escaping from a tire. On a signal from your director, stop the air, and notice the breath support from the diaphragm.

3. Imagine that as you inhale you are filling a balloon with air. Inhale over 8 counts, exhale on a "ss."

ARTICULATION

In our daily speech we are often careless about pronouncing all the sounds of all the words:

I gotta go home now. Are ya goin' t' the dance? Who ya goin' with?

In choral singing, however, it's important to articulate the diction clearly. Otherwise the performance will sound ragged and sloppy. Here are a few exercises to practice articulation. Speak each phrase first, then sing it on a repeated unison pitch or scale pattern.

"t" and "d"

Both consonants are produced with the tip of the tongue, but "t" is "unvoiced" and "d" is "voiced." Notice that sometimes the "t" sound is used even when there is no "t" in the word: *laughed* is pronounced *laft.*

4. Repeat the following "t" patterns:
   - *t t t t t t t t*
   - *Tiptoe through the tulips*
   - *Two times ten is twenty*
   - *He laughed. She talked. We worked. They hoped.*

5. Repeat the following:
   - *d d d d d d d*
   - *day by day*
   - *dream a dream*
   - *do or die*

TEACHING SUGGESTIONS

Essential Elements:
- The student will develop good diction through the articulation of consonants. (NS 1A)

Focus:
Pronounce "t" and "d" consonants clearly.

Teaching Tips:
- Present the information about "t" and "d" articulation as stated in the student text p. 130 and 131.
- Speak each phrase on exercise 4 and 5, and ask students to echo.
- Repeat exercises 4 and 5 on a unison pitch or a unison scale pattern.
- Review the articulators (lips, teeth, tongue) with students. Encourage students to exaggerate the lip, teeth and tongue movement for these exercises.

ARTICULATION

"t" and "d" before a vowel

When "t" or "d" is followed by a syllable or word beginning with a vowel, connect the "t" with that vowel:

- *What a surprise!*
- *Wait until tomorrow.*
- *Sweet is the sound.*
- *The winding road*
- *Open the window*
- *Ride off into the sunset*

"t" and "d" before a consonant

Even though in speaking, we often drop a "t" or "d" before a consonant, singing it that way would sound careless. Practice these consonant sounds, followed by the same sound on a short phrase:

- *t-b, t-b, t-b*   *might belong, might belong*
- *t-d, t-d, t-d*   *sweet dessert, sweet dessert*
- *t-f, t-f, t-f*   *Is it free? Is it free?*
- *d-m, d-m, d-m*   *We could meet you there.*
- *d-th, d-th, d-th*   *Sound the trumpet*

"t" followed by another "t" — "d" followed by another "d"

Most of the time when a "t" or "d" is followed by another "t" or "d", you will want to pronounce only one of them.

- *I went to see the doctor.*
- *Come at ten o'clock.*
- *We had a great time.*
- *Pretty as a picture*
- *Written on the wall*
- *Hey diddle diddle, the cat and the fiddle*

"t" followed by an "s"

Most of the time, you will want to connect the "t"with the "s".

- *sweet song*
- *great sound*
- *street sign*
- *Mozart sonata*
- *short story*

"Tall vowels communicate the beauty of the musical line. Precise consonants communicate the meaning of the text."

Teaching Tips: (continued)

- *This page presents more exercises focusing on clear, crisp consonants.*
- *Practice these exercises using the model/echo procedure.*

Extension:
Transfer the articulation of isolated consonants (t, d) to actual words sung in music being performed.

EIGHTH NOTES AND RESTS

So far, we've used whole, half, and quarter notes. An *eighth note* (♪) is half the value of a quarter note. Two eighth notes (♫) have the same duration as one quarter note. The eighth note has a corresponding rest, the eighth rest (♪) which shares the same length as an eighth note.

Below is a chart summarizing the notes and rests we've learned.

	note	rest
whole	o	—
half	♩	—
quarter	♩	𝄽
eighth	♪	♪

The following diagram summarizes the relationships between the notes we've studied:

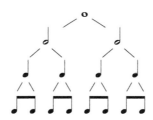

More about eighth notes

If the quarter note receives the beat, you can consider eighth notes to be a division of the beat:

Beat: ♩ ♩ ♩ ♩

Division: ♫ ♫ ♫ ♫

Eighth notes may be notated singly with a stem and a flag:

Or they may be beamed together in groups:

Check your knowledge!

1. How many *eighth notes* equal a quarter note? A half note? A whole note?

2. Describe two ways eighth notes can be notated.

TEACHING SUGGESTIONS

Essential Elements:
• The student will recognize and apply eighth note rhythm notation. (NS 5C, 5D)

Focus:
Eighth notes are a division of the beat when the quarter note gets the beat.

Teaching Tips:
• Review whole, half, and quarter notes and rests.
• Introduce eighth notes and eighth rests using the information presented on student p. 132.
• Ask students to keep the beat (quarter note) by tapping, and at the same time speak the eighth note division using your selected counting system. Do not omit this step. Students will need practice in feeling that the eighth note is a division of the beat.

• See the appendix on teacher page 189 which presents the most commonly used counting systems. It is important that you select a counting system and use it consistently.
• Answers to Check Your Knowledge! section are located within the text on this page.

RHYTHM PRACTICE

Read each line (clap, tap, or chant).

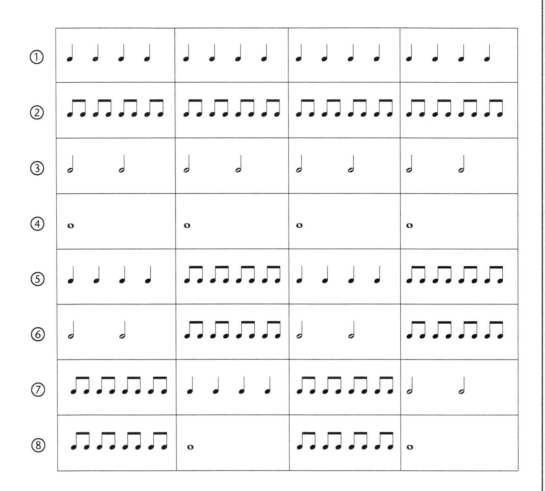

Teaching Tips: *(continued)*

• *Read each line.*
• *Perform the lines consecutively, simultaneously or in canon. For fun, try turning the page upside down and performing it that way. Start at the end and perform backwards. The idea is to give students as much practice at keeping a steady beat and performing the division of the beat as possible.*

EIGHTH NOTE PRACTICE

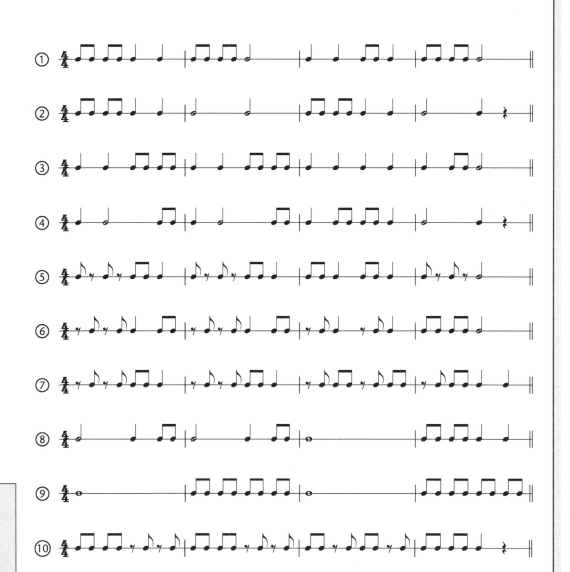

"Keep the beat and division steady. Do not rush! Do not rush! Do not rush!"

TEACHING SUGGESTIONS

Essential Elements:
- The student will read and perform rhythm patterns of eighth notes and rests accurately. (NS 5A)
- (Extension) The student will compose short rhythm compositions. (NS 4A)
- (Extension) The student will improvise short melodies over repeated rhythm patterns played on rhythm instruments. (NS 3C)

Focus:
Perform rhythms with precision.

Teaching Tips:
- Sight-read each line using your chosen counting method.
- Pay special attention to eighth notes on the off beat such as exercises 6, 7, and 10.
- Set a metronome to the eighth note and see if students can stay with the divided beat.
- Read several lines consecutively, or divide singers into groups and perform two or more lines simultaneously.

Extension:
- Encourage students to create and notate their own rhythm exercises adding the use of eighth notes and eighth rests. Perform the compositions in class.
- Improvise short melodies above the repeated student-composed rhythm patterns.

SPEECH CHORUS

History: *Hey Diddle Diddle!* is an English nursery rhyme. Sometimes these rhymes are called "Mother Goose" rhymes, but no one knows exactly why. We don't know who made them up or when they began. Rhymes for little children like this one exist in many different languages and cultures around the world.

As you prepare to perform *Hey Diddle Diddle!*
• Read the rhythm of each part.
• Combine the parts.
• Add the text. Repeat to increase the tempo.
• Add the dynamics, and concentrate on the articulation and diction, especially the "t" and "d" sounds.

Hey Diddle Diddle!

For 2-Part Speech Chorus

English Nursery Rhyme

Music by
EMILY CROCKER

TEACHING SUGGESTIONS

Essential Elements:
• The student will combine text and rhythm.
   (NS 1E)

Focus:
Voice inflection and dynamics add interest to a
   speech chorus.

Teaching Tips:
• Read the suggestions on student p. 135 and
   follow carefully.
• Make sure the eighth note divisions are steady
   and even. Do not let the eighth notes sound like
   dotted rhythms.
• Dynamic contrast and crisp articulation are
   essential to the performance of this piece.
• Do not rush.
• Have fun with the contrasts in this piece.

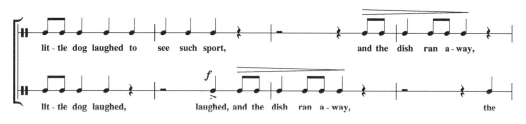

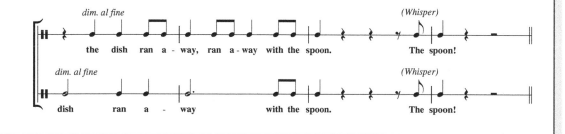

TEACHING SUGGESTIONS

Essential Elements:

• *(Extension) The student will arrange a nursery rhyme or other poem for speech chorus. (NS 4B)*

Extension:

• *Encourage students to notate other nursery rhymes or other short poems for speech chorus. Perform for the class.*

EE18: GOALS AND OVERVIEW

This review chapter allows you to evaluate the students' learning of eighth notes and rests, and also allows for additional practice of eighth notes within a melodic context.

In addition, three performance songs are included to allow the students to apply their musical skills in both sight-reading and performance situations. In this chapter treble choirs are offered the option of singing SSA, and tenor bass choirs have the option of singing TTB. Encourage your choirs to take this challenge, and expand their musical growth.

ESSENTIAL ELEMENTS AND NEW CONCEPTS

Voice:
The student will review diphthongs and articulation. (NS 1A)

• Review diphthongs and other aspects of articulation.

Theory:
The student will review rhythmic values of eighth, quarter, half and whole notes and rests in $\frac{2}{4}$, $\frac{3}{4}$ and $\frac{4}{4}$ meter. (NS 5C, 5D)

• Rhythm review and practice

Sight-Reading:
The student will review rhythmic and melodic patterns in the key of F major. (NS 1E)

• Combinable exercises in the key of F

Performance:
The student will apply music reading skills to an a cappella song in the key of F major. (NS 5A, 5B, 5E)
The student will become familiar with the stylistic markings in the songs which follow. (NS 5C)
The student will practice good articulation in an a cappella song. (NS 1A)

• SSA, TTB, and SATB a cappella songs in the key of F major which use eighth notes.

REVIEW AND PRACTICE

1. What is a *diphthong*?

2. Describe how to sing the vowel sounds in the following diphthongs:
   I   my   day   joy   now   way   though

3. How do you perform the "t" or "d" in the following phrases?
   - *Wait until dark*
   - *The winding road*

4. In the following phrases, how do you sound the "t" or "d" when singing?
   - *Great day!*
   - *Sound the trumpet*

5. In the following phrases with double "t" or "d" sounds, do you sound both of them when singing?
   - *Hey diddle diddle*
   - *Come at ten o'clock*

6. How do you perform a "t" or "d" followed by an "s"?
   - *Sweet sounds*
   - *Ends so soon*

Apply your knowledge by singing the following exercises:

TEACHING SUGGESTIONS

Essential Elements:
- The student will review diphthongs and articulation. (NS 1A)

Focus:
Review the vocal technique information presented in chapters 16-17.

Teaching Tips:
- Answer the questions on this page in large groups or cooperative learning situations.

Answers: *(Page numbers refer to the student text.)*
1. A diphthong is a combination of two vowel sounds. *(p. 118)*
2. I = ah(ee)
   my = mah(ee)
   day = deh(ee)
   joy = jaw(ee)
   now = nah(oo)
   way = (oo)eh(ee)
   though = thoh(oo) *(p. 118)*

3. Connect the "t" and "d" sounds with the vowels that follow. *(p. 131)*
4. Sound both "t" and "d" in both words. *(p. 131)*
5. No. You do not sound double "t's" or double "d's" when singing. *(p. 131)*
6. Connect the "t" or "d" with the "s" which follows. *(p. 131)*

- Apply your knowledge of d and t consonants to singing words by performing exercises 1-3.

REVIEW AND PRACTICE

Check your knowledge!

1. How many beat(s) does an eighth note receive in a meter of $\frac{4}{4}$?

2. How many eighth notes take up a whole measure of $\frac{3}{4}$ meter? $\frac{2}{4}$ meter? $\frac{4}{4}$ meter?

3. How many quarter notes take up a whole measure of $\frac{3}{4}$ meter? $\frac{2}{4}$ meter? $\frac{4}{4}$ meter?

4. How many half notes take up a whole measure of $\frac{3}{4}$ meter? $\frac{2}{4}$ meter? $\frac{4}{4}$ meter?

5. What number of eighth notes equals the duration of a half note? A whole note?

6. What one note value completely fills a measure of $\frac{4}{4}$ meter? Of $\frac{3}{4}$? Of $\frac{2}{4}$?

7. What note value receives the beat in $\frac{4}{4}$ meter?

8. How many beats does a whole rest receive in $\frac{4}{4}$ meter? A half rest? A quarter rest? An eighth rest?

9. Assuming a meter of $\frac{3}{4}$, how many eighth notes are in the song *Happy Birthday to You*?

10. Supply a meter for the following rhythm patterns:

TEACHING SUGGESTIONS

Essential Elements:
• *The student will review rhythmic values of eighth, quarter, half and whole notes and rests in $\frac{2}{4}$, $\frac{3}{4}$ and $\frac{4}{4}$ meter. (NS 5C, 5D)*

Focus:
Review the rhythmic values presented in chapters 1-17.

Teaching Tips:
• *Answer the questions on this page in large group or cooperative learning situations.*

Answers: *(Page numbers refer to the student text.)*
1. *An eighth note receives 1/2 beat in $\frac{4}{4}$ meter. (p. 132)*
2. *Six eighth notes = one measure in $\frac{3}{4}$ meter. Four eighth notes = one measure in $\frac{2}{4}$ meter. Eight eighth notes = one measure in $\frac{4}{4}$ meter. (p. 132)*
3. *Three quarter notes = one measure in $\frac{3}{4}$ meter. Two quarter notes = one measure in $\frac{2}{4}$ meter. Four quarter notes = one measure in $\frac{4}{4}$ meter. (p. 132)*
4. *One half note + one beat = one measure in $\frac{3}{4}$ meter. One half note = one measure in $\frac{2}{4}$ meter. Two half notes = one measure in $\frac{4}{4}$ meter. (p. 132)*
5. *Four eighth notes = one half note. Eight eighth notes = one whole note. (p. 132)*
6. *A whole note completely fills a $\frac{4}{4}$ measure. A dotted half note completely fills a $\frac{3}{4}$ measure. A half note completely fills a $\frac{2}{4}$ measure. (p. 121)*
7. *Quarter note receives the beat in $\frac{4}{4}$ meter. (p. 132)*
8. *A whole rest = four beats in $\frac{4}{4}$ meter. A half rest = two beats in $\frac{4}{4}$ meter. A quarter rest = one beat in $\frac{4}{4}$ meter. An eighth rest = 1/2 beat in $\frac{4}{4}$ meter. (p. 132)*
9. *Eight eighth notes are in Happy Birthday (unless the name of the birthday person has multiple syllables.) (p. 132)*
10. *Reading left to right: $\frac{3}{4}$, $\frac{4}{4}$, $\frac{2}{4}$, $\frac{4}{4}$, $\frac{2}{4}$, $\frac{4}{4}$, $\frac{4}{4}$, $\frac{3}{4}$, $\frac{2}{4}$*

PRACTICE WITH EIGHTH NOTES

Read each line separately and in any combination. Decribe the time and key signature.

TEACHING SUGGESTIONS

Essential Elements:
- The student will review rhythmic and melodic patterns in the key of F major. (NS 1E)

Focus:
Apply music reading skills in reading melodies which use eighth notes.

Teaching Tips:
- Sight-read each line using your established sight-reading procedures.
- Combine any line with any other line when the unison lines are secure.
- Encourage all singers to sing all lines. Changing voices may find more success with lines 2, 4, 5, and 7. New baritones may find more success with line 8.
- Notice that every line does not start on the keynote F. Establish starting pitch of each line before singing .
- Always encourage students to sing musically, even when sight-reading.

TREBLE CHORUS

History: In the late 19th and early 20th century, interest began to grow in folk music. Cecil Sharpe in the British Isles, John Jacob Niles and John Lomax in the United States, Bela Bartok and Zoltan Kodály in Hungary, and others traveled back roads and country lanes writing down tunes sung by the people they met along the way.

As the work of these musical pioneers became known, composers began to use folk music as source material for symphonies, ballet scores, operas, songs and chamber music. In America, Aaron Copland and Virgil Thomson were two well-known composers who made use of American folk music. In Hungary, Kodály, in addition to his work in cataloging folk music and composing, became known as a leader in music education. *Let Us Chase The Squirrel* is an example of a simple American folksong arranged using Kodály techniques.

As you prepare to perform *Let Us Chase The Squirrel*:
- Discover which sections are monophonic, which are homophonic, and which are polyphonic.
- Identify the key, and notice the places where there are interval skips. Take special care to distinguish the descending intervals from the tonic: F to E, and F to C.
- Read the rhythm of each part, then add the pitch. When the parts are secure, combine them into two (or optionally three) parts.
- Add dynamics and perform expressively.

Let Us Chase The Squirrel
For SA or SSA a cappella

TEACHING SUGGESTIONS

Essential Elements:
- The student will apply music reading skills to an a cappella song in the key of F major. (NS 5A, 5B, 5E)
- The student will become familiar with the stylistic markings in the songs which follow. (NS 5C)
- The student will practice good articulation in an a cappella song. (NS 1A)

Focus:
Perform an a cappella song in the key of F major using precise articulation.

Teaching Tips:
- Note that the treble choir song and performance suggestions appear on student p. 140, the tenor bass song and suggestions are on student p. 142, and the mixed choir song and teaching suggestions are on student p. 144.
- Ask your treble choirs to read and discuss the historical information about folk music on student p. 140.
- Sight-read "Let Us Chase the Squirrel" using your established sight-reading procedure.
- Establish and maintain a steady beat while rehearsing the staggered entrances. Remind students not to rush the eighth notes.
- Follow the suggestions as presented on p. 140.

Teaching Tips: (continued)

- After the rhythm and pitch of the song are secure, begin using the text. Pay special attention to articulation.
- Attempt to perform the song with clean articulation at the tempo marked. Do not choose a faster tempo than can be performed effectively.

Student Book Page **142**

TENOR BASS CHORUS

History: Sea Chanteys were songs sung by sailors in rhythm with their work. Work on board a ship was very hard, and different kinds of songs developed for pulling ropes and other tasks.

Leave Her, Johnny is a variation of two earlier sea chanteys: *Leave Her, Bullies, Leave Her* and *Across the Western Ocean*. The song dates to about 1850 when thousands left Ireland after the potato famine forced them to flee the economic hardship of their native land.

As you prepare to perform *Leave Her, Johnny*:
- Identify the key and time signatures, and notice where the melody has interval skips.
- Read the rhythm, then add pitch, and repeat until the parts are secure.
- Sing in two (or optionally three) parts, and add the text. Sing with expression.

Leave Her, Johnny

For TB or TTB a cappella

Traditional Sea Chantey

Arranged by
EMILY CROCKER

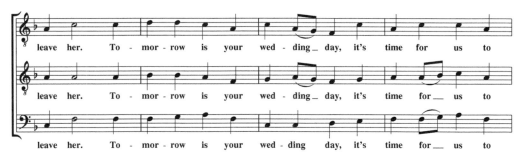

Teaching Tips: *(continued)*

- *Note that the treble choir song and performance suggestions appear on student p.140, the tenor bass song and suggestions are on student p. 142, and the mixed choir song and teaching suggestions are on student p. 144.*
- *Ask the students to read and discuss the historical information about sea chanteys on student p. 142.*
- *Sight-read "Leave Her, Johnny" using your established sight-reading procedure.*

- *Establish and maintain a steady beat while singing eighth note patterns.*
- *Follow the teaching suggestions as presented on student p. 142.*

Teaching Tips: (continued)

- After the rhythm and pitch of the song are secure, begin using the text. Pay special attention to singing diphthongs correctly.
- Sing musically, with attention given to tall vowels.
- Note that this song may be performed effectively with two parts (Tenor I and Bass) or three parts as written.

Extension:

- Ask students to name other sea chanteys with which they are familiar. Sea chanteys appearing in the Essential Elements for Choir Series are "Blow Ye Winds" and "Boatmen Stomp."

MIXED CHORUS

This traditional rhyme has been set to music in such a way that the humor of the text is emphasized. As you prepare to perform Betty Botter:
- Notice the places where the melody outlines the intervals of the tonic chord.
- Notice the 2- measure rest in both the SA and TB. Be sure to count and listen to the other parts so you come in on the right pitch at the right time.
- Chant the text in rhythm, concentrating on articulation. Use expression!

Betty Botter

Essential Elements:
- *(Extension) The student will arrange a tongue twister or other short rhyme for speech chorus using varied dynamic or other style markings. (NS 4B)*

Teaching Tips: *(continued)*

- *Note that the treble choir song and performance suggestions appear on student p.140, the tenor bass song and suggestions are on student p. 142, and the mixed choir song and teaching suggestions are on p. 144.*

- *Ask the choir to sight-read "Betty Botter" using your established sight-reading procedure.*
- *Establish and maintain a steady beat while singing eighth note patterns.*
- *Follow the teaching suggestions as presented on student p. 144.*
- *Do not add text until the pitch and rhythm of the song are secure.*
- *When adding text, start with a slow tempo, concentrating on crisp, clear articulation.*
- *Gradually increase tempo, but always choose a tempo at which singers can perform effectively.*

- *Pay special attention to dynamic contrasts and performing processes articulation at all dynamic levels.*

Extension:
- *Encourage singers to create songs or speech choruses using other tongue twisters. Remind them to add dynamic changes for interest.*

EE19: GOALS AND OVERVIEW

In many parts of the country, singing the consonant "r" is a challenge. This lesson gives you the opportunity to focus on singing "r" in such a way that it does not overly "color" the vowel sound which surrounds it. Certainly, one lesson in one book will not do the job of fixing this continual choral ensemble problem. Use this chapter as an opportunity to focus on this issue, and encourage your students to listen critically to all the music they perform for good diction, including the "r" consonant.

In addition, this lesson features some changing meter exercises and songs.

ESSENTIAL ELEMENTS AND NEW CONCEPTS

Voice:
The student will develop the posture and breath control needed to support choral tone. (NS 1A)
The student will articulate the "r" consonant correctly. (NS 1A)

• The consonant "r"

Theory:
The student will read and perform rhythm patterns in various meters. (NS 5A)

• Meter, downbeat

Sight-Reading:
The students will read and perform rhythms in changing meter. (NS 1E)

• Rhythm exercises using changing meters.

Performance:
The student will perform an a cappella song with changing meter. (NS 1E)
The student will apply music reading skills to an a cappella song using changing meter. (NS 5A, 5B, 5E)
(Extension) The student will compare changing meter examples from Western art music, African polyrhythmic percussion, and Indian tabla.

• Perform an SA, TB, or SATB a cappella song in the key of F major which uses changing meters.

POSTURE/BREATH

Posture: Check your posture and ask yourself these questions.
• Stand with feet apart (Is your weight balanced?)
• Knees unlocked (Can you bend them easily?)
• Back straight (Are you standing erect comfortably and not stiff?)
• Head erect (Is your chin level, and not too far up or down?)
• Rib cage lifted (Is your chest high and able to expand?)
• Shoulders relaxed (Are they comfortably down, not too far forward or back?)
• Hands at your side (Are they relaxed and free of tension?)

Remember that just like athletes, singers need to prepare themselves for the physical process of singing. Performance, whether on the playing field or in a concert will suffer if the body is not sufficiently prepared or involved.

Practice good posture, good breathing, and good vocal habits every day in rehearsal, and these good habits will be there to help you succeed in performance.

1. Lift the left shoulder high and let it fall. Repeat with the right shoulder and finally both shoulders. Stretch overhead, fall forward like a rag doll, and gradually stand up to a good singing posture.

Breath: Practice breathing exercises every day. Apply this practice to all your music making, sight-reading music, rehearsing music, performing music.

2. When people are suddenly startled, they usually take a deep natural breath very quickly. Take a "surprised" breath. Notice the action of the *diaphragm*.

3. Imagine that there is an elevator platform at the bottom of your lungs. Drop the platform toward the floor as you inhale. Inhale 4 counts, exhale 4 counts. Repeat with 5, then 6 counts.

ARTICULATION
Singing the consonant "r"
There are two kinds of "r" sounds which are used in singing in English. The American "r" is the "r" which is used in daily speech. The flipped "r" could be described by the saying "very good" sounding as "veddy good" as they say it in England (the tip of the tongue at the back of the front teeth). Both are used in singing.

In singing, we must carefully prepare the articulation of words containing "r" sounds. This is because an "r" can affect the vowel sound which it precedes or follows. Say or sing the word "care" on a unison pitch, holding the vowel and gradually changing to the "r" sound: "kehrrrrrr _____". Did you notice the movement of the tongue and the change in the sound?

TEACHING SUGGESTIONS

Essential Elements:
• *The student will develop the posture and breath control needed to support choral tone. (NS 1A)*
• *The student will articulate the "r" consonant correctly. (NS 1A)*

Focus:
The consonant "r" requires special attention.

Teaching Tips:
• *Student page 145 and 146 should be presented in the same lesson.*
• *Read and discuss the material on the "r" consonant on p. 145 and 146.*
• *Demonstrate the American "r" and the flipped "r" as presented on p. 146. Ask students to echo.*
• *If students are unable to flip or roll the r, suggest they practice saying "Betty" repeatedly until it sounds like "beddy." Then repeatedly say "beddy" faster and faster until it begins to sound like a flipped or rolled r.*

• *Perform the "care" exercise as presented on student p. 145 slowly so that singers understand the effect that "r" has on the vowel sound.*

ARTICULATION

Guidelines for singing "r"

Whether you choose to sing an American "r" or a flipped "r" will depend on the kind of music you are singing. It is important, however, for an ensemble to have a uniform sound on an "r", since even 1 or 2 voices can affect the sound of the entire group.

Sing "r" before a vowel: This holds true whether the "r" is in the same word with the vowel, or in adjoining words. Practice the following examples and repeat at different pitch levels.

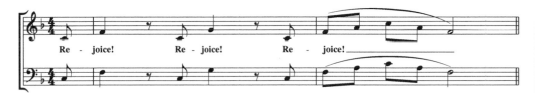

Re - joice!   Re - joice!   Re - joice! _____

De-emphasize "r" before a consonant: This can be a challenging concept for anyone learning to sing, but a necessary one in developing a pleasing choral tone quality. There are some exceptions to this practice, mostly in popular music and certain kinds of solo work, but in general, the rule applies. Practice the following examples, omitting the "r" sound when it precedes a consonant.

Star - light,   star   bright,   first   star   I   see   to - night.
Stah   lah(ee)t,   stah   brah(ee)t,   fuhst   stahr   ah(ee)   see   too - nah(ee)t

---

Teaching Tips: *(continued)*

- *When singing an "r" before a vowel, articulate the "r" and quickly move to the vowel. Avoid "singing on the r."*
- *Follow the suggested procedures about an "r" before a consonant as presented on p. 146. The exercises on 146 will help the choir grasp this concept.*

MORE ABOUT METER

Remember that *meter* is a form of rhythmic organization. In the simple meters we have been using, the top number indicates the number of beats per measure in the music. The bottom number indicates which note value receives the beat.

4	=	Four beats per measure (♩ ♩ ♩ ♩)
4	=	The quarter note (♩) receives the beat
3	=	Three beats per measure (♩ ♩ ♩)
4	=	The quarter note (♩) receives the beat
2	=	Two beats per measure (♩ ♩)
4	=	The quarter note (♩) receives the beat

So that the ear can easily recognize and group notes into the various meters, each meter stresses certain beats. Almost all meters stress the first beat of each measure. This is called the downbeat.

In $\frac{4}{4}$ meter, a secondary stress occurs on beat three along with the stressed downbeat.

Check your knowledge!
1. Define *meter*.

2. Describe the following meters: $\frac{3}{4}$, $\frac{2}{4}$, $\frac{4}{4}$.

3. What is a *downbeat*?

4. What beats are stressed in $\frac{4}{4}$ meter? In $\frac{3}{4}$ meter? In $\frac{2}{4}$ meter?

TEACHING SUGGESTIONS

Essential Elements:
• The student will read and perform rhythm patterns in various meters. (NS 5A)

Focus:
Most meters stress the first beat of each measure (downbeat).

Teaching Tips:
• Review $\frac{2}{4}$, $\frac{3}{4}$, and $\frac{4}{4}$ meter as presented on student p. 147.
• Practice the examples, stressing the first beat of each measure.
• This information prepares students for the changing meter sight-reading and performance examples which follow.
• Review the information by discussing the Check Your Knowledge! questions. All answers may be found within the text on this page.

CHANGING METERS

Read the following exercise with changing meters. Clap, tap, or chant.

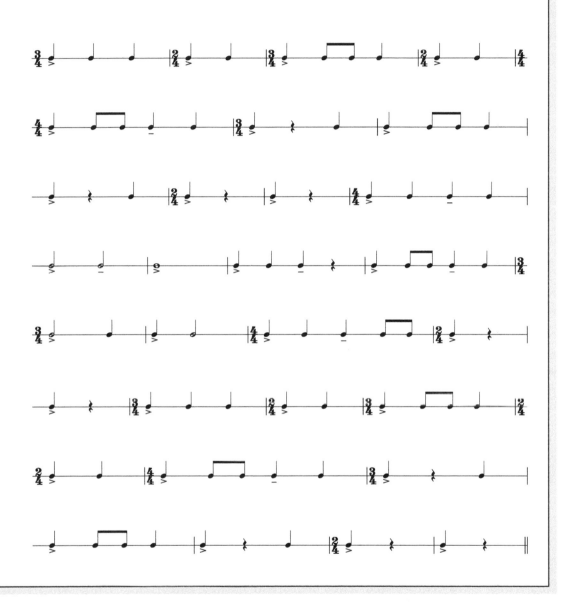

TEACHING SUGGESTIONS

Essential Elements:
• The students will read and perform rhythms in changing meter. (NS 1E)

Focus:
The beat stays constant even though meter and stressed beats change.

Teaching Tips:
• Sight-read the changing meter rhythm drill using your established counting system.
• Remind students to accent the downbeat of each measure.
• Initially read at a slow tempo. Gradually increase tempo, but do not allow students to accelerando. Maintain a steady tempo.
• Practicing this page with a metronome will help maintain a steady tempo.

Extension:
• Challenge your students to conduct this changing meter exercise.

TREBLE • TENOR BASS • MIXED

History: Music with changing meters has been widely used throughout history and in various cultures. During the Renaissance, meters shifted easily from meter groupings of 2 beats to groupings of 3. During the period from 1600-1900 metrical patterns became more regular, although Bach, Beethoven, Brahms, and others used techniques which interrupted the regular pulse. Brahms wrote a famous work *Variations*, Op. 21, No.2 which was written in $\frac{3}{4}$ + $\frac{4}{4}$.

By the 20th century, composers became interested in more variety in rhythm and meter as a compositional technique. Works for all kinds of ensembles were written with changing meters and other interesting rhythmic effects. There are many famous works which use changing meters including Igor Stravinsky's *Danse sacral* from *The Rite of Spring* and Carl Orff's *Carmina Burana*.

Music from other cultures including music of the Middle East, Eastern Europe and Indian ragas are often organized with complex meters and other rhythmic devices.

As you prepare to perform *Alleluia*:
• Identify the time signatures throughout the piece. Identify the key.
• Read through the rhythm. Stress the downbeats and other secondary beats in each measure as they occur.
• Notice the places where the melody outlines the intervals of tonic chord. Can you identify the tonic chord when it occurs?
• Add the pitch, and repeat as needed for accuracy.
• Add the text, and work to increase the tempo. (De-emphasize the "r" in the word "together," i.e. sing as *too-GEH-thuh*)
• Sing with energy and expression.

Alleluia
For SA, TB, or SATB a cappella

Music by
JOHN LEAVITT

TEACHING SUGGESTIONS

Essential Elements:
• The student will perform an a cappella song with changing meter. (NS 1E)
• The student will apply music reading skills to an a cappella song using changing meter. (NS 5A, 5B, 5E)

Focus:
Perform an a cappella song using changing meter.

Teaching Tips:
• Note that "Alleluia" p. 149-151 can be sung by treble choirs (sing SA), tenor bass (sing TB) or mixed choirs (sing SATB).
• Read and discuss the information about changing meters throughout history as presented on p. 149.
• Follow the suggested teaching sequence on p. 149 to learn "Alleluia."

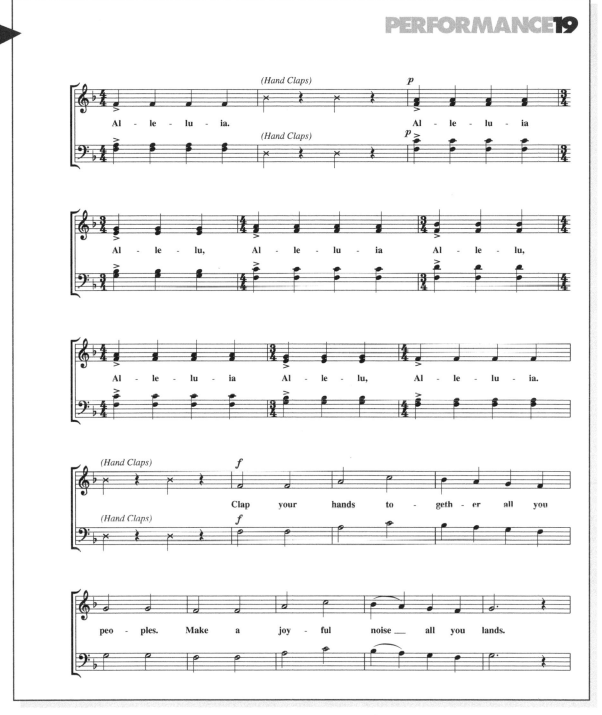

Essential Elements:
- *(Extension) The student will compare changing meter examples from Western art music, African polyrhythmic percussion, and Indian tabla.*

Teaching Tips: *(continued)*

- *After rhythms and pitches are secure, add text. Pay special attention to the tall vowels on the word "alleluia."*
- *Remind students to follow the dynamic markings carefully.*
- *Even when singing softly, the downbeats must be stressed.*

- *Rehearse "Alleluia" slowly and gradually increase tempo. Maintain a steady tempo throughout. Do not rush to the end.*

Extension:
- *Listen to recordings of the changing meter examples mentioned on student p. 150:* **The Rite of Spring**, **Carmina Burana**, *Brahms'* **Variations**. *If possible, include music from other cultures, most notably Africa and India.*

EE20: GOALS AND OVERVIEW

This chapter serves as a comprehensive review of the material in Chapters 1-19 along with providing a culminating musical experience that allows the students to apply their musical skills.

If the students have mastered this volume successfully, they may move into *ESSENTIAL MUSICIANSHIP - Book 2*, which reviews and practices the material in Book 1, and extends the learning into more complex musical skills and knowledge. The first several chapters of Book 2 provide additional practice with new musical material.

ESSENTIAL ELEMENTS AND NEW CONCEPTS

Voice:
The student will review aspects of breathing, posture, and vocal technique. (NS 1A)

• Comprehensive review of chapters 1-19

Theory:
The student will describe and review elements of musical notation. (NS 5C, 5D)

• Comprehensive review of chapters 1-19

Performance:
The student will apply music reading skills in the performance of a choral piece. (NS 1E)

• Perform an SA, TB, or SATB accompanied song in the key of F major.

VOICEBUILDERS20

COMPREHENSIVE REVIEW

Answer the following questions orally in large or small group discussion.

1. Why is good posture important in singing?

2. Describe the steps for a good singing posture.

3. Describe a good singing posture for singing from memory. Describe a good singing posture for holding music. For sharing music with another singer.

4. Why do we need *articulation* in singing? What are the *articulators*?

5. What are the three stages of breathing for singing?

6. Describe the action of the *diaphragm* during breathing. The abdomen. The ribs. The lungs.

7. How does an expanded rib cage affect breath capacity?

8. What are the five basic vowel sounds? Describe the basic formation of each.

9. What is the general rule for producing other vowel sounds in addition to the five basic vowel sounds?

10. What is the *neutral* vowel?

11. Describe the difference in the vowel sounds of the following:
   • 2nd syllable of *welcome*
   • 1st syllable of *Alleluia*

12. What is the source of *vocal tone*? What is it popularly called?

13. How do the vocal folds produce sound?

14. What is a *diphthong*? Describe and demonstrate how to sing the following diphthongs: *light   bright   you   I   why   now*

15. Describe and demonstrate the pronunciation of the following words using the consonants "t", "d", and "r":
   Dream a dream   Sweet music   Rejoice!   Dark brown is the river

TEACHING SUGGESTIONS

Essential Elements:
• The student will review aspects of breathing, posture, and vocal technique. (NS 1A)

Focus:
Review information learned in Chapters 1-19.

Teaching Tips:
• Answer the questions on page 152 orally or in small groups.

Answers: (Page numbers refer to the student text.)
1. Steps for good singing are: stand with feet apart, knees unlocked, back straight, head erect, rib cage lifted, shoulders relaxed, hands at your side. (p. 1)
2. Good posture helps produce good breathing. (p. 1)
3. Singing from memory: See number 1. Singing while holding music: Hold music up and out from the body so head is erect and aligned with the spine, hold elbows out and away from the body, turn to face the conductor. Singing while sharing music: hold music up and away from body; turn so both singers are facing the conductor. (p. 52)
4. Articulation is the pronunciation of the consonants. The three main articulators are the lips, teeth and tongue. (p. 52)
5. The three stages of breathing are inhalation, exhalation and release. (p. 69)
6. Diaphragm muscle contracts, flattens and moves downward. The abdomen moves outward. The ribs move outward. The lungs expand. (p. 69)
7. An expanded rib cage increases breath capacity. (p. 1)

8, The five basic vowels sounds are "ee, eh, ah, oh, oo." The basic formation is a relaxed jaw, space inside the mouth, and a vertical mouth shape. (p. 5)
9. The general rule for producing other vowel sounds is to sing the vowel sound as you would say it, but modify the vowel by keeping a relaxed jaw, maintaining vertical space in the mouth, keeping the corners of the mouth from spreading outward. (p. 88)
10. A neutral vowel is also called a schwa and refers to an "uh" sound on an unstressed word or syllable. (p. 96)
11. The second syllable of "welcome" is an unstressed neutral vowel and the 1st syllable of "alleluia" is a stressed "ah" vowel. (p. 96)

12. The source of vocal tone is the larynx. It is popularly called the voice box. (p. 80)
13. The vocal folds produce sound by exhaling air between the vocal chords causing them to vibrate. (p. 80)
14. A diphthong is a combination of two vowel sounds. (p. 118) light = lah(ee)t, bright = brah(ee)t, you = (ee)oo, I= ah(ee), why = (oo)ah(ee), now = nah(oo). (p. 118)
15. Dream a dream: connect the "d" to the vowel that precedes it; sweet music: sound both the "t" and the "m" which follows; rejoice: flipped "r"; dark brown is the river: American "r" in "river". (p. 131)

THEORY BUILDERS 20

COMPREHENSIVE REVIEW

Check your knowledge!

1. What is *rhythm*?

2. Define *beat*.

3. How many half notes equal the same duration as a whole note?

4. How many quarter notes equal the same duration as a half note?

5. How many quarter notes equal the same duration as a whole note?

6. How many lines and spaces make up a *staff*?

7. Give both names for the *clefs* we've learned and describe them.

8. Name the pitch which may be written on its own little line in either clef.

9. When treble clef notes are written in the bass clef or bass clef notes are written in the treble clef, they use additional little lines as in #8. What are these lines called?

10. What are the vertical lines that divide a staff into smaller sections called?

11. Name the smaller divided sections of a staff.

12. How can you tell the end of a section or piece of music?

13. Describe *meter*.

14. What are the numbers that identify the meter called?

15. Describe the following meters: $\frac{4}{4}$, $\frac{3}{4}$, $\frac{2}{4}$

16. What is another name for musical notes?

17. Define *scale*. What is the Italian word for scale and its definition?

18. Describe *key*. Describe *keynote*.

19. What is the difference between a *whole step* and a *half step*?

TEACHING SUGGESTIONS

Essential Elements:
• The student will describe and review elements of musical notation. (NS 5C, 5D)

Focus:
Review information learned in Chapters 1-19.

Teaching Tips:
• Answer the questions in large or small discussion groups.
• Page 153 and 154 should be covered in a single lesson.

Answers: (Page numbers refer to the student text.)

1. Rhythm is organization of sound lengths (duration). (p. 2)
2. Beat is a steadily recurring pulse. (p. 2)
3. Two half notes = a whole note. (p. 2)
4. Two quarter notes = a half note. (p. 2)
5. Four quarter notes = a whole note. (p. 2)
6. Five lines and 4 spaces make a staff. (p. 7)
7. G clef = Treble clef. F clef = bass clef. A clef is a symbol that identifies a set of pitches (p. 7)
8. Middle C may be written on its own little line in either staff. (p. 7) .
9. Ledger lines are little lines written in either staff. (p. 55)
10. The vertical lines which divide a staff are called bar lines. (p. 12)

11. The smaller divided sections of a staff are called measures. (p. 12)
12. A double bar ends a section or piece of music. (p. 12)
13. Meter is a form of rhythmic organization. The numbers which identify meter are called a time signature. (p. 12)
14. The numbers which identify the meter are called the time signature. (p. 12)
15. $\frac{4}{4}$ =four beats per measure, quarter note receives the beat; $\frac{3}{4}$ =three beats per measure, quarter note receives the beat; $\frac{2}{4}$ = two beats per measure, quarter note receives the beat. (p. 12)
16. Pitch is another name for musical notes. (p. 24)

17. A scale is an inventory or collection of pitches. The Italian word "scala" means ladder. (p. 24)
18. Key is the importance of one pitch over the others in a scale. The keynote is the home tone. (p. 24)
19. A half step is smallest distance or interval between two notes on a keyboard. A whole step is a combination of two half steps side by side. (p. 33)
20. A major scale is a specific arrangement of whole steps and half steps. (p. 33)

COMPREHENSIVE REVIEW

20. What is a *major scale*?

21. What is the order of whole/half steps in a major scale?

22. What is a *slur*?

23. Where does the word *pianoforte* come from and what does it mean?

24. Describe *f p mf mp*. What are these signs called?

25. What is an octave?

26. Define *soprano, alto, tenor, bass*.

27. What is an *interval*? What is the difference between *melodic* and *harmonic* intervals?

28. What is a *chord*?

29. How many tones are needed to form a chord?

30. What is the difference between a *chord* and a *triad*?

31. What is another name for *keynote*?

32. On what tone of the major scale is a tonic chord built?

33. Describe the key signature for C major, G major, and F major.

34. How many beat(s) does an eighth note receive in a meter of $\frac{4}{4}$?

35. What number of eighth notes equals the duration of a half note? A whole note?

36. What is a *downbeat*?

37. What beats are stressed in $\frac{4}{4}$ meter? In $\frac{3}{4}$ meter? In $\frac{2}{4}$ meter?

38. What is the dotted note rule?

Answers: *(continued)*

21. The order of major scale whole steps and half steps is whole, whole, half, whole, whole, whole, half. (p. 33)

22. A slur is a curved line placed above or below a group of notes to indicate that they are to be sung on the same syllable. A slur is also used to indicate that a group of notes are to be performed legato. (p. 36)

23. Pianoforte comes from Italy and means soft-loud. (p. 15)

24. F means forte (loud), p means piano (soft) (p. 48) Mf means mezzo forte (medium loud), and mp means mezzo piano (medium soft). (p. 58) These terms are called dynamic markings. (p. 58)

25. An octave is the distance between eight scale tones. (p. 35)

26. Soprano is the highest treble voice, usually written in treble clef. Alto is a treble voice that is lower than the soprano, usually written in treble clef.
Tenor is a male voice written in bass or treble clef. Bass is a male voice that is lower than a tenor, written in bass clef. (p. 26)

27. An interval is a measurement between two pitches. (p. 81) Melodic intervals are intervals sounded in succession. (p. 81) Harmonic intervals are sounded simultaneously. (p. 89)

28. A chord is two or more harmonic intervals combined. (p. 89)

29. Three or more tones are needed to form a chord. (p. 91)

30. A chord is the combination of three or more tones played or sung simultaneously. A triad is a three-note chord built in thirds over a root tone. (p. 97)

31. Another name for keynote is tonic. (p. 97)

32. A tonic chord is built on the keynote or tonic. (p. 97)

33. Key signature for C major = no sharps or flats. Key signature for G major = 1 sharp (F#). Key signature for F major = 1 flat (Bb). (p. 64 and 21)

34. An eighth note receives 1/2 beat in $\frac{4}{4}$ meter. (p. 132)

35. Four eighth notes = one half note. Eight eighth notes = one whole note. (p. 132)

36. A downbeat is the stressed first beat of each measure. (p. 147)

37. Beats one and three are stressed in $\frac{4}{4}$ meter. Beat one is stressed in $\frac{3}{4}$ meter. Beat one is stressed in $\frac{2}{4}$ meter. (p. 147)

38. The dotted note rule is that a dot receives half the value of the note to which it is attached. (p. 121)

TREBLE CHORUS

Oh, Soldier, Soldier

For SA and Piano

Traditional Text

Music by
EMILY CROCKER

TEACHING SUGGESTIONS

Essential Elements:
• The student will apply music reading skills in the performance of a choral piece. (NS 1E)

Focus:
Perform a full-length song as a culminating project to celebrate the completion of this course of study.

Teaching Tips:
• Note that the treble song "Oh Soldier, Soldier" appears on student p. 155-158; the tenor bass song "The Hunt" appears on student p. 159-161; and the mixed song, "The Bells" appears on 162-165.
• Sight-read "Oh Soldier, Soldier" using your established method of sight-reading.
• Establish and maintain the steady beat while singing the eighth note patterns. Do not rush.
• Note unison and harmony sections. Stress the need for perfect unisons in the frequent unison sections.
• Add text after pitch and rhythm are secure.

• Remind students to utilize all they have learned about breathing, diction, tall vowels, consonants, articulation, word stress, and stylistic markings as they perform this song.
• Challenge students to perform "Oh Soldier, Soldier" to the best of their ability. This may be used as an evaluation tool.

Higher Level Thinking:
• Remind students that any time they apply previous learning to a new situation they are using higher level thinking skills. Encourage them to transfer learning to new situations on a daily basis.

TREBLE CHORUS

no, sweet maid, I can-not mar-ry thee, for I have no coat to put on." Then up she went to her
  (hat)
  (boots)

no, sweet maid, I can-not mar-ry thee, for I have no coat to put on." Then up she went to her
  (hat)
  (boots)

grand - fa-ther's chest, and got him a coat of the ver - y best. "Oh
  (hat)
  (some boots)

grand - fa-ther's chest, and got him a coat of the ver - y best. "Oh
  (hat)
  (some boots)

TREBLE CHORUS

TREBLE CHORUS

TENOR BASS CHORUS

The Hunt

For TB and Piano

Traditional American (adapted)

Music by
EMILY CROCKER

Teaching Tips: (continued)

- *Note that the treble song "Oh Soldier, Soldier" appears on student p. 155-158; the tenor bass song "The Hunt" appears on student p. 159-161; and the mixed song, "The Bells" appears on 162-166.*
- *Sight-read "The Hunt" using your established method of sight-reading.*
- *Establish and maintain the steady beat while singing the eighth note patterns. Do not rush.*
- *Add text after pitch and rhythm are secure.*
- *Accurate diphthongs may be a challenge in this piece, especially on the "ay" vowel.*

- *Remind students to utilize all they have learned about breathing, diction, tall vowels, consonants, articulation, word stress, and stylistic markings as they perform this song.*
- *Challenge students to perform "The Hunt" to the best of their ability. This may be used as an evaluation tool.*

Higher Level Thinking:

- *Remind students that any time they apply previous learning to a new situation they are using higher level thinking skills. Encourage them to transfer learning to new situations on a daily basis.*

TENOR BASS CHORUS

cho - rus, let's ush - er in the day. The sport's ex - ceed - ing

glo - ri - ous, a - rise, make no de - lay. The sun shines now up -

a - rise, make no de - lay, de - lay.

TENOR BASS CHORUS

on us, come a - way, come a - way, come a - way__ make no de -

Come a - way, a - way, come a - way, a - way,

lay.   A - way,__ oh __ come a - way.

MIXED CHORUS

The Bells

For SATB and Piano

Words by
EDGAR ALLEN POE

Music by
JOHN LEAVITT

Teaching Tips: *(continued)*

- *Note that the treble song "Oh Soldier, Soldier" appears on student p. 155-158; the tenor bass song "The Hunt" appears on student p. 159-161; and the mixed song, "The Bells" appears on 162-166.*
- *Sight-read "The Bells" using your established method of sight-reading.*
- *Establish and maintain the steady beat while singing the eighth note patterns. Do not rush.*
- *Add text after pitch and rhythm are secure.*
- *Precise articulation may be a challenge in this piece, especially on the staggered entrances.*

- *Remind students to utilize all they have learned about breathing, diction, tall vowels, consonants, articulation, word stress, and stylistic markings as they perform this song.*
- *Encourage basses to imitate a bell sound by emphasizing the first consonant (d) and going quickly to the "ng" of "ding, dong."*
- *Challenge students to perform "The Bells" to the best of their ability. This may be used as an evaluation tool.*

Higher Level Thinking:

- *Remind students that any time they apply previous learning to a new situation they are using higher level thinking skills. Encourage them to transfer learning to new situations on a daily basis.*

MIXED CHORUS

Student
Book Page
164

MIXED CHORUS

MIXED CHORUS

SOLFEGE

(Movable "do")
"Do" changes as the key changes.

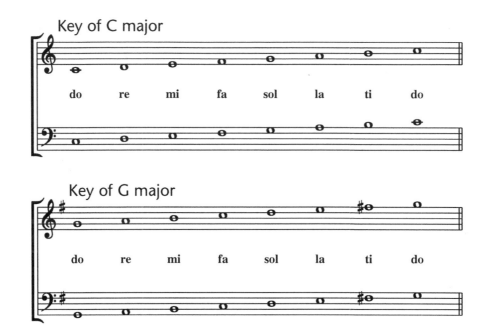

Movable "do" — Accidentals (in all keys)

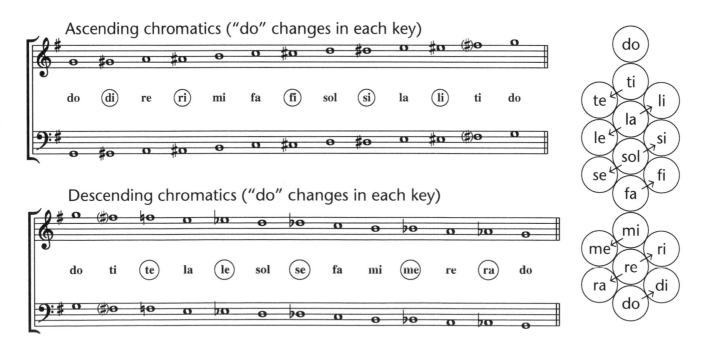

SOLFEGE

(Fixed "do")
"Do" is C and the pitch syllables remain fixed no matter what the key.

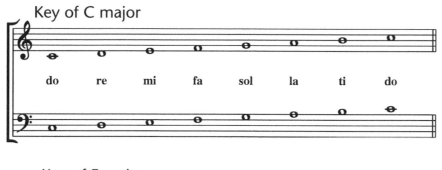

Key of C major

do re mi fa sol la ti do

Key of F major

fa sol la te do re mi fa

Fixed "do"
Accidentals are fixed as follows:

Ascending chromatics

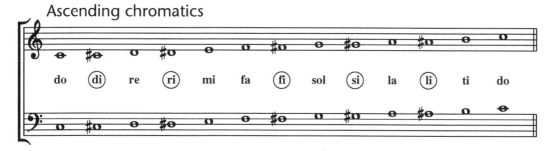

do (di) re (ri) mi fa (fi) sol (si) la (li) ti do

Descending chromatics

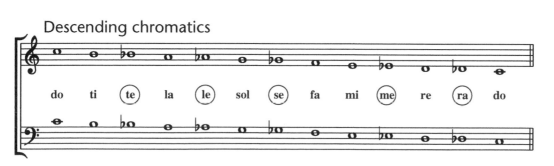

do ti (te) la (le) sol (se) fa mi (me) re (ra) do

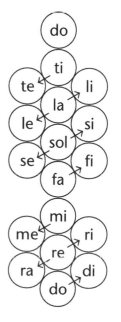

NUMBERS

Numbers (pitch)
Like movable "do," the "1" changes with each key.

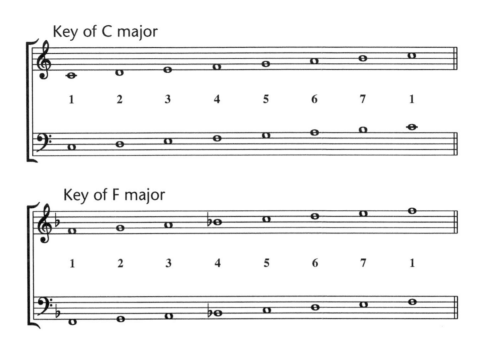

Accidentals can be performed either by singing the number but raising or lowering the pitch by a half step, or by singing the word "sharp" or "flat" before the number as a grace note.

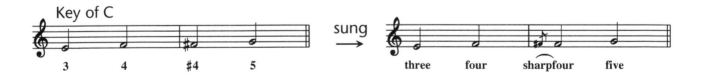

COUNTING SYSTEMS - SIMPLE METER

There are several systems in use which are quite effective. Here are three:

Kodály	Traditional	Eastman
ta ta ta ta	1 2 3 4	1 2 3 4
ta_____ ta_____	1_____ 3_____	1_____ 3_____
ta_____	1_____	1_____
ti ti ti ti ti ti ti ti	1 & 2 & 3 & 4 &	1 te 2 te 3 te 4 te
ti ri ti ri ti ri ti ri ti ri ti ri ti ri ti ri	1 e & a 2 e & a 3 e & a 4 e & a	1 ta te ta 2 ta te ta 3 ta te ta 4 ta te ta
ti ti ri ti ti ri ti ti ri ti ti ri	1 & a 2 & a 3 & a 4 & a	1 te ta 2 te ta 3 te ta 4 te ta

COUNTING SYSTEMS

Kodály	Traditional	Eastman
(Beat) ti ri ti ti ri ti ti ri ti ti ri ti	1 e & 2 e & 3 e & 4 e &	1 ta te 2 ta te 3 ta te 4 ta te
(Beat) ta ___ ta	1 ___ 4	1 ___ 4
(Beat) ta i ti ta i ti	1 ___ & 3 ___ &	1 ___ te 3 ___ te
(Beat) tim ri tim ri tim ri tim ri	1 a 2 a 3 a 4 a	1 ta 2 ta 3 ta 4 ta
(Beat) tir im tir im tir im tir im	1 e 2 e 3 e 4 e	1 ta 2 ta 3 ta 4 ta
(Beat) ta ta ta ta ___ ta ___	1 2 3 4 ___ 3 ___	1 2 3 4 ___ 3 ___
(Beat) ta ta ___ ta	1 2 ___ 4	1 2 ___ 4
(Beat) syn - co - pa syn - co - pa (or ti ta ti)	1 & ___ & 3 & ___ &	1 te ___ te 3 te ___ te
(Beat) tir im ri tir im ri tir im ri tir im ri	1 e a 2 e a 3 e a 4 e a	1 ta ta 2 ta ta 3 ta ta 4 ta ta

OTHER SIMPLE METERS

Adapt the information from the charts on pages 189-190 to apply to music in other simple meters:

Simple Meters: Simple meters are based upon the note which receives the beat, i.e. $\frac{4}{4}$ meter is based upon the quarter note receiving the beat.

2 = 2 beats per measure (♪ ♪)
8 = The eighth note (♪) receives the beat

3 = 3 beats per measure (♪ ♪ ♪)
8 = The eighth note (♪) receives the beat

4 = 4 beats per measure (♪ ♪ ♪ ♪)
8 = The eighth note (♪) receives the beat

2 = 2 beats per measure (♩ ♩)
2 = The half note (♩) receives the beat (Note: sometimes written as ¢ "cut time")

3 = 3 beats per measure (♩ ♩ ♩)
2 = The half note (♩) receives the beat

4 = 4 beats per measure (♩ ♩ ♩ ♩)
2 = The half note (♩) receives the beat.

COMPOUND METER

Kodály	Traditional	Eastman

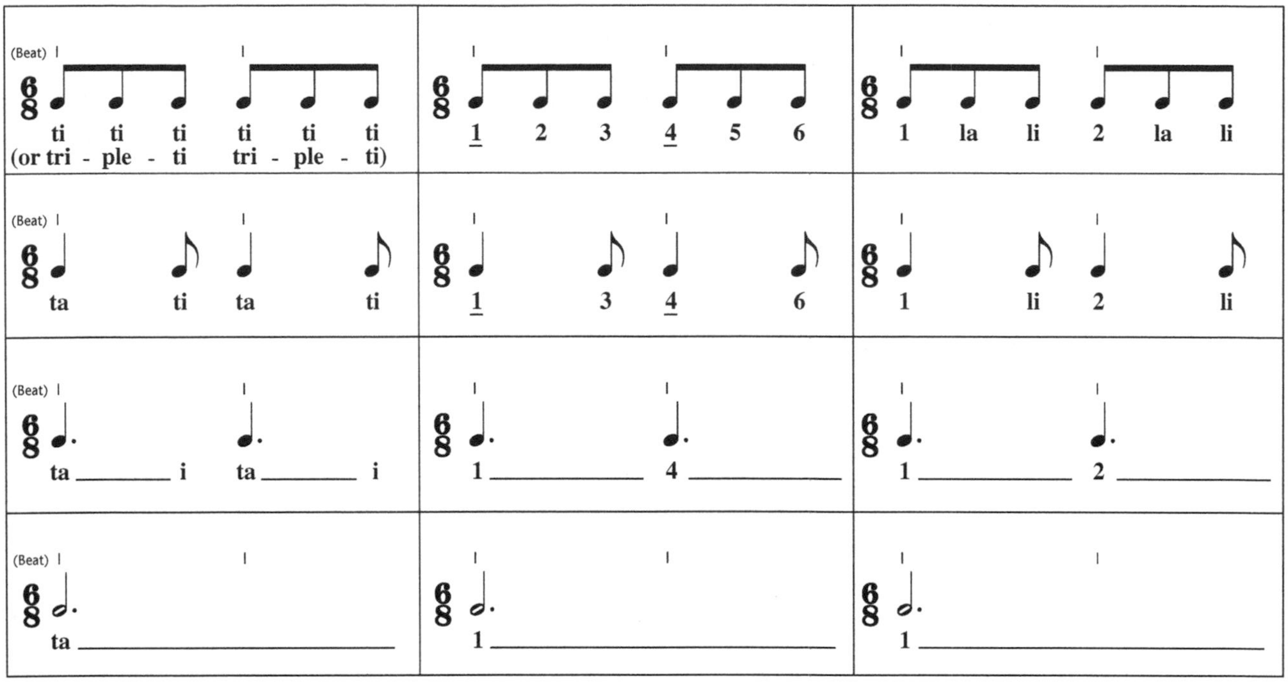

(Beat)

6/8 ti ti ti ti ti ti (or tri-ple-ti tri-ple-ti)

6/8 1 2 3 4 5 6

6/8 1 la li 2 la li

6/8 ta ti ta ti

6/8 1 3 4 6

6/8 1 li 2 li

6/8 ta____i ta____i

6/8 1_____4_____

6/8 1_____2_____

6/8 ta_____

6/8 1_____

6/8 1_____

OTHER COMPOUND METERS

Adapt the information from the above charts to apply to music in other compound meters.

Compound Meters: Compound meters are meters which have a multiple of 3, such as 6 or 9 (but not 3 itself). Unlike simple meter which reflects the note that receives the beat, compound meter reflects the note that receives the division.

To determine the note that receives the beat, add three divisions together. For example:

6 = 6 divisions to the measure (2 groups of 3)
8 = The eighth note receives the division
    (the dotted quarter receives the beat)

9 = 9 divisions to the measure (3 groups of 3)
8 = The eighth note receives the division
    (the dotted quarter receives the beat)

12 = 12 divisions to the measure (4 groups of 3)
4 = The quarter note receives the division
    (the dotted half note receives the beat)

An exception to this compound meter rule is when the music occurs at a slow tempo, then the music is felt in beats, rather than divisions.

RHYTHM DRILLS

Simple Meter
The rhythmic, melodic, and harmonic exercises on the following pages are included for reference or drill as needed.

Beat, Division, and Subdivision
Clap, tap, or chant each line

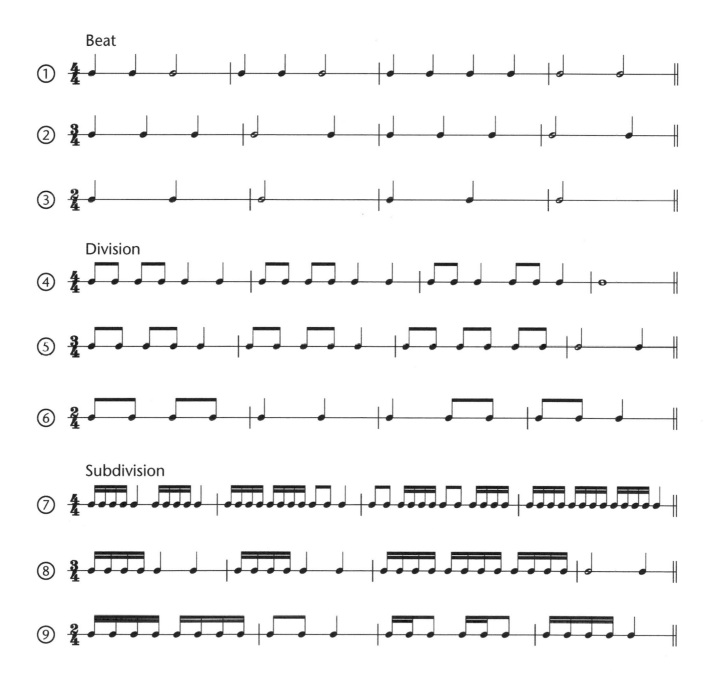

RHYTHM DRILLS

Dotted Rhythms
Clap, tap, or chant each line

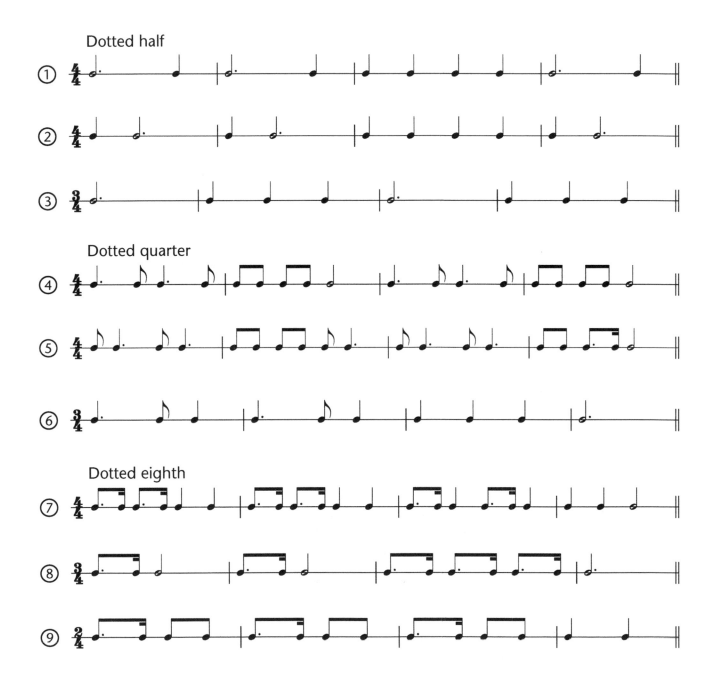

RHYTHM DRILLS

Compound Meter
Clap, tap, or chant each line.
What note gets the beat? The division?

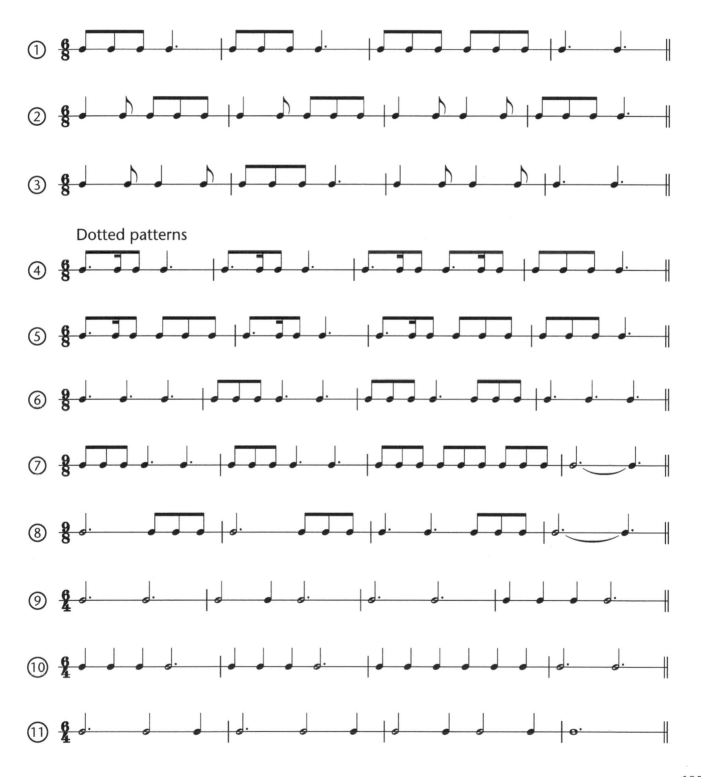

Dotted patterns

PITCH DRILLS

Key of D Major

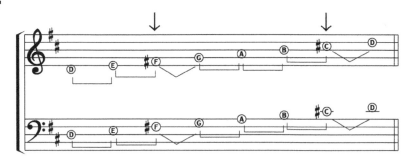

Chord–builders

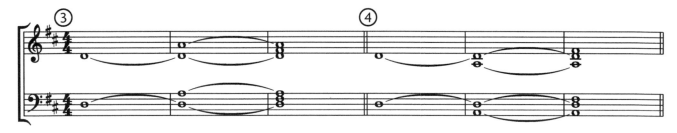

Chord Drills

Sing separately and in any combination.

PITCH DRILLS

Key of B Flat Major

Chord-builders

Chord Drills

Sing separately and in any combination.

CAREERS IN MUSIC

Studying music allows people to develop aesthetic awareness in the arts along with the lifelong skills of self-discipline, team work, goal-setting, self-expression, problem solving, self-confidence and much more.

The following outline and suggested activities provide students with the opportunity of learning about diverse careers in music. By discussing these topics, you may increase the possibility that your students will become patrons of the arts, regardless of their chosen career. Use these ideas as a starting point for class discussion and projects in the exploration of music careers.

Music Education
- Choral director (church, school, community)
- Elementary music specialist
- Band or orchestra director
- Private studio (piano, voice, instrumental)
- College/University Professor (piano, voice, instrumental, history, theory, composition, conducting, education)

Suggested Activity: You are the professional choral role model for your students. Discuss your decision to become a choral director. Invite other music teachers from your district or nearby university to present a brief presentation for the class.

Music Therapy
- Music therapist

Suggested Activity: Invite a music therapist to describe their profession to your class. If possible, observe a music therapist at work in your community.

Music Merchandising
- Sheet music retailers
- Instrument retailers
- Record/CD retailers

Suggested Activity: Take a field trip to a local sheet music, instrument, or record store.

Music Manufacturing
- Musical instruments
- Recording/electronic equipment
- Record/CD manufacturing
- Related music items
- Instrument repair
- Piano tuning

Suggested Activity: Invite a manufacturer's representative to your class to discuss their company's variety of products and the techniques used in the manufacturing process.

Composition
- Choral, Band, Orchestral Composer/Arranger
- Vocal or Solo Instrumental Composer/Arranger
- Movie Soundtracks/Background music composer
- TV/Commercial jingle writer
- Pop music composer
- Specialty arranger

Activity: Ask students to do research projects on composers and arrangers of the music they are learning in class. Invite a composer from your area to speak to the class or institute a composer-in-residence project. Discuss the skills and preparation necessary for becoming a professional composer. Encourage interested students to develop their composition/improvisation skills.

Conducting
- Choral Conductor (school, university, church, community, professional)
- Band or Orchestra Conductor (school, university, church, community, professional)
- Music Theater Conductor

Activity: Arrange to take a field trip to an area performance (professional, community, school, or university) or open rehearsal. Try to arrange a "meet the conductor" session for your choir at a festival or honors chorus event. Visit your local media center for videos, books, and films which examine the lives and careers of conductors. Teach your students the conducting patterns and allow them the opportunity of conducting the choir in rehearsal or performance.

Music/Sound Production
- Recording studio engineer
- Producer
- Sound technician for concerts or other live performances

Activity: Visit a local recording studio, or visit your local media center for videos, books, and films which show the recording process. Parents or other amateur enthusiasts in your community may be able to provide a demonstration for your class.

Music Performance
- Jazz/blues/rock/pop/country singer or instrumentalist
- Opera or recital singer
- Studio singer or instrumentalist
- Symphony or chamber music instrumentalist
- Church musician
- Music theater performer or instrumentalist
- Dance accompanist

Activity: Invite a variety of professional musicians to visit your class to speak about their work. A source for professional musicians might be your local university.

Music Publishing
- Music editor
- Engraver
- Graphic artist
- Typesetter
- Sales

Activity: Visit a music publisher's exhibit at your next state or national convention. They may have catalogs or promotional materials which you may share with your students. Your school or some of your students may have music software which can be used for engraving. Examine books and music style manuals to become familiar with industry standards for music notation.

Music Business and other related fields
- Manager of a concert hall or a performing group
- Copyright or Entertainment lawyer
- Music industry professionals
- Acoustical engineer or architect

Activity: Acquaint your students with the copyright law and how it affects them personally and as part of a school music organization. Ask the manager of your local concert hall or civic concert series to speak to your class.

BIBLIOGRAPHY

Alderson, Richard. *Complete Handbook of Voice Training*. West Nyack, New York: Parker Publishing Co., Inc., 1979.

Baker, Theodore, ed. *Schirmer Pronouncing Pocket Manual of Musical Terms*. 4th ed., rev. by Nicolas Slonimsky. New York: Schirmer Books, 1978.

___. *Baker's Biographical Dictionary of Musicians*. 6th ed., rev. by Nicolas Slonimsky. New York: Schirmer Books, 1978.

Bartle, Jean A. *Lifeline for Children's Choir Directors*. London: Oxford Press, 1988.

Bjorneberg, Paul, ed. *Exploring Careers in Music*. Reston, Virginia: Music Educators National Conference, 1990.

Claghorn, Charles Eugene. *Biographical Dictionary of American Music*. West Nyack, New York: Parker Publishing, Co., 1973.

Coffin, Berton. *Overtones of Bel Canto*. Metuchen, New Jersey: The Scarecrow Press, 1980.

Collins, Don L. *Teaching Choral Music*. Englewood Cliffs, New Jersey: Prentice-Hall, 1993.

Consortium of National Arts Education Associations. *National Standards for Arts Education: What Every Young American Should Know and Be Able to Do in the Arts*. Reston, Virginia: Music Educators National Conference, 1994.

Cooksey, John M. "The Development of a Contemporary, Eclectic Theory for the Training and Cultivation of the Junior High School Male Changing Voice." Parts 1-4. *Choral Journal* 18:2-5 (1977-78).

Decker, Harold A., and Julius Herford, eds. *Choral Conducting Symposium*. 2nd ed. Englewood Cliffs, New Jersey: Prentice Hall, Inc., 1988.

De Angelis, Michael. *The Correct Pronunciation of Latin According to Roman Usage*. St. Gregory Guild, Inc., 1965.

Downs, Philip G. *Classical Music: The Era of Haydn, Mozart, and Beethoven*. New York: W.W. Norton & Company, Inc., 1992.

Ehmann, Wilhelm, and Frauke Haasemann. *Voice Building for Choirs*. Chapel Hill, North Carolina: Hinshaw Music, Inc., 1982.

Ehret, Walter, and George K. Evans. *The International Book of Christmas Carols*. Englewood Cliffs, New Jersey: Prentice-Hall, 1963.

Ewen, David. *All the Years of American Popular Music*. Englewood Cliffs, New Jersey: Prentice-Hall, Inc., 1977.

___. *The Complete Book of Classical Music*. Englewood Cliffs, New Jersey: Prentice-Hall, Inc., 1966.

___. *The World of Twentieth Century Music*. Englewood Cliffs, New Jersey: Prentice-Hall, Inc., 1968.

Feitz, Leland. *Cripple Creek! A Quick History of the World's Greatest Gold Camp*. Colorado Springs, Colorado: Little London Press, 1967.

Gackle, Lynn. "The Adolescent Female Voice: Characteristics of Change and Stages of Development." *Choral Journal* 31(8)(1991): 17-25.

Grout, Donald J., and Claude V. Palisca. *A History of Western Music*. 4th ed. New York: W.W. Norton & Company, Inc., 1988.

Grun, Bernard. *The Timetables of History*. 3rd ed. New York: Simon & Schuster, 1991.

Haasemann, Frauke, and James M. Jordan. *Group Vocal Techniques*. Chapel Hill, North Carolina: Hinshaw Music Inc., 1991.

Hoffer, Charles R. *Teaching Music in the Secondary Schools*. 4th ed. Belmont, California: Wadsworth Publishing, Co., 1991.

Jeffers, Ron. *Translations and Annotations of Choral Repertoire*. Vol. 1, Sacred Latin Texts. Corvallis, Oregon: Earthsongs, 1988.

Johnston, Richard. *Folk Songs North America Sings*. Toronto: E. C. Kerby, Ltd., 1984.

Kennedy, Michael. *The Concise Oxford Dictionary of Music*. 3rd ed. Oxford, England: Oxford University Press, 1980.

Lamb, Gordon H. *Choral Techniques*. 3rd ed. Dubuque, Iowa: Wm. C. Brown Company Publishers, 1988.

Lomax, Alan. *The Folk Songs of North America.* Garden City, New York: Doubleday & Company, Inc., 1975.

Marshall, Madeleine. *The Singer's Manual of English Diction.* New York: Schirmer Books, 1953.

May, Wiliiam V., and Craig Tolin. *Pronunciation Guide for Choral Literature: French, German, Hebrew, Italian, Latin, Spanish.* Reston, Virginia: Music Educators National Conference, 1987.

Music Educators National Conference, Committee on Standards. *Guidelines for Performances of School Music Groups: Expectations and Limitations.* Reston, Virginia: Music Educators National Conference, 1986.

Music Educators National Conference, Task Force on Choral Music Course of Study. *Teaching Choral Music: A Course of Study.* Reston, Virginia: Music Educators National Conference, 1991.

Morgan, Robert P. *Twentieth-Century Music: A History of Musical Style in Modern Europe and America.* New York: W.W. Norton & Company, Inc., 1991.

New York State School Music Association. *NYSSMA Manual: A Resource Manual of Graded Solo & Ensemble Music, Suitable for Contests and Festivals.* Westbury, New York: New York State School Music Association, 1991.

Palisca, Claude V., ed. *Norton Anthology of Western Music, Vol. I.* New York: W. W. Norton & Company, 1980.

Pfautsch, Lloyd. *English Diction for Singers.* New York: Lawson Gould, Inc., 1971.

Plantiga, Leon. *Romantic Music: A History of Musical Style in Nineteenth-Century Europe.* New York: W.W. Norton & Company, Inc., 1984.

Randel, Don M., ed. *The New Harvard Dictionary of Music.* Cambridge, Massachusetts: The Belknap Press of Harvard University Press, 1986.

Rao, Doreen. *We Will Sing: Choral Music Experience.* New York: Boosey & Hawkes, 1993.

___, ed. *Choral Music for Children: An Annotated List.* Reston, Virginia: Music Educators National Conference, 1990.

Robinson, Ray and Allen Winold. *The Choral Experience.* New York: Harper's College Press, 1976.

Roe, Paul F. *Choral Music Education.* 2nd ed. Englewood Cliffs, New Jersey: Prentice-Hall, Inc., 1983.

Runfola, Maria, ed. *Proceedings of the Symposium on the Male Adolescent Changing Voice.* Buffalo, New York: State University of New York at Buffalo Press, 1984.

Sandburg, Carl. *The American Songbag.* New York: Harcourt Brace Jovanovich, Inc., 1955.

Sadie, Stanley, ed. *The New Grove Dictionary of Music and Musicians.* Washington D.C.: Grove's Dictionaries of Music, 1980.

Shaw, Kirby. *Vocal Jazz Style.* 2nd ed. Milwaukee, Wisconsin: Hal Leonard Corporation, 1987.

Stanton, Royal. *Steps to Singing for Voice Classes.* 2nd ed. Belmont, California: Wadsworth Publishing Company, Inc., 1976.

Ulrich, Homer. *A Survey of Choral Music.* New York: Harcourt Brace Jovanovich, Inc., 1973.

University Interscholastic League. *Prescribed Music List for Bands, Orchestras and Choirs.* University Interscholastic League, 1991-1994.

Uris, Dorothy. *To Sing in English.* New York: Boosey and Hawkes, 1971.

Vennard, William. *Singing, the Mechanism and the Technique.* New York: Carl Fischer, 1988.

Wall, Joan Robert Caldwell, Tracy Gavilanes, and Sheila Allen. *Diction for Singers: A Concise Reference for English, Italian, Latin, German, French, and Spanish Pronunciation.* Dallas: PST ...Inc., 1990.

Young, Carlton R. *Companion to the United Methodist Hymnal.* Nashvillle, Tennessee: Abingdon Press, 1993.

RECOMMENDED VIDEOS

Archibeque, Charlene, *Daily Workout for a Beautiful Voice: Featuring Charlotte Adams.* Santa Barbara, California: Santa Barbara Music Publishing.

Ehly, Eph. *Choral Singing Style.* Milwaukee, Wisconsin: Hal Leonard Corporation.

___. *Excellence in Conducting "The Natural Approach."* Milwaukee, Wisconsin: Hal Leonard Corporation.

___. *Positive Motivation for the Choral Rehearsal.* Milwaukee, Wisconsin: Hal Leonard Corporation.

___. *Tuning the Choir.* Milwaukee, Wisconsin: Hal Leonard Corporation.

Hassemann, Frauke, and James Jordan. *Group Vocal Technique.* Chapel Hill, North Carolina: Hinshaw Music.

Jacobson, John. *John Jacobson's Riser Choreography.* Milwaukee, Wisconsin: Hal Leonard Corporation.

Nelson, Charles, Austin King, and Jon Ashby. *The Voice: Three Professionals Discuss the Function, Abuses and Care of the Most Important Instrument of Communication.* Abilene, Texas: Voice Institute of West Texas at Abilene Christian University.

Wall, Joan, and Robert Caldwell. *The Singer's Voice: Breath.* Dallas, Texas: Pst...Inc.

___. *The Singer's Voice: Vocal Folds.* Dallas, Texas: Pst...Inc.

___. *The Singer's Voice: Vocal Tract.* Dallas, Texas: Pst...Inc.

___. *The Singer's Voice: Acoustics.* Dallas, Texas: Pst...Inc.